AF265185

Dictionary
Lao Zi's
Dao De Jing

Dr. Auke Schade

nemonik-thinking.org

Yin-Yang

nemonik-thinking.org

Copyright

Copyright © January 2018 by Dr. Auke Schade. All rights reserved. This copy of (Schade, Dictionary Lao Zi's Dao De Jing, 2018) is for private use only. This copy or any part thereof shall not be resold, reproduced, or transmitted in any form or by any means, electronic or mechanical, including photocopying, recording, or otherwise, or placed in any public information storage and retrieval system, including the Internet, without a prior written permission from the copyright owner.

First Edition 2 January 2018
@ nemonik-thinking.org
ISBN 978-0-473-42677-4

Acknowledgement

I am greatly indebted to Xiandong Meng. His insight in Chinese culture and language provided significant support in compiling this dictionary concerning the pictographs mentioned in the different versions of Lao Zi's *Dao De Jing*.

Abstract

This Chinese-English and English-Chinese dictionary is especially compiled for the translation of Lao Zi's ancient book *Dao De Jing* (Schade, Meta-translation Lao Zi's Dao De Jing (1-37), 2018) and (Schade, Meta-translation Lao Zi's Dao De Jing (38-81), 2018). *Dao De Jing* means literally—*A Classic about the Way of Nature and the Way of People.* It aims to maximize your success, which is to obtain what you seek and escape what you suffer. Success is maximized by aligning the *Way of People* with the *Way of Nature* (Schade, Stunning Revelations about Lao Zi's Dao De Jing, 2017). The Chinese versions used in this study include— (Wang Bi, 226-249 AD); (He-Shang Gong, 179-157 BC); (Fu Yi, ~200 BC); (Mawangdui (A), ~200 BC); (Mawangdui (B), ~200 BC); and (Guodian, ~300 BC). Together, those versions contain about 1,600 different pictographs. Every language changes over time and, therefore, some of Lao Zi's ancient pictographs are not used anymore, while the meaning of others has changed. In addition, most modern Chinese pictographs have several English meanings that foster ambiguity. Therefore, the exhaustive English meanings for each pictograph were extracted from reputable sources. Furthermore, a system of *Digital Index for Pictographs (DIP)* is introduced that simplifies the digital classification of Chinese pictographs.

Free eBook @
nemonik-thinking.org

nemonik-thinking.org

nemonik-thinking.org

Dr. Auke Schade

My life started during the devastation of World War II. As a teenager, I worked as a carpenter and studied building engineering at night school. During the seventies, I became a financial manager for a multinational corporation, ran my own business, and studied economics in my spare time. My interest in the psychology of management extended to the interaction between the mind, body, and reality. In 1980, I immigrated to New Zealand where I obtained a doctorate in psychology from the University of Auckland. My mission is to make people the smartest thinkers they can be, which has led me to the development of nemonik thinking (Schade, Think Smarter with Nemonik Thinking, 2016).

Download free eBooks and videos @
nemonik-thinking.org

nemonik-thinking.org

Yin-Yang

Contents

nemonik-thinking.org

Contents

Yin-Yang

nemonik-thinking.org

DIGITAL INDEX PICTOGRAPHS (DIP)

Copyright DIP

This book introduces a digital coding system for identifying Chinese pictographs called—*Digital Index for Pictographs* hereafter referred to as *DIP*. Copyright © January 2018 by Dr. Auke Schade. All rights reserved. This copyright of DIP includes any alternative comprising different pictograph strokes, number of DIP digits, and language. DIP or any part thereof shall not be resold, applied, reproduced, or transmitted in any form or by any means, electronic or mechanical, including photocopying, recording, or otherwise, or placed in any public information storage and retrieval system, including the Internet, without a prior written permission from the copyright owner.

Description DIP

The location of each digit in the six-digit DIP code represents a different type of pictograph stroke i.e.

$$- \ | \ / \ \backslash \ \mathsf{J} \ \mathsf{L}$$

The actual number of a particular DIP code in each digit location represents the number of identical strokes, while zero (0) indicates the lack of the particular stroke in that pictograph. For example: 〇 = 000000; 囗 = 220000; 人 = 001100; and 儿 = 001001. Nine (9) or more identical strokes in a pictograph are indicated as nine (9). Hence, the potential DIP codes ranges from 000000 to 999999. It is proposed that DIP is simpler and less ambiguous than the traditional identification of Chinese pictographs with radicals or Pinyin. Application of DIP does not require knowledge of the Chinese language or pictographs. The number of digits in the DIP code is flexible and could be increased or decreased. DIP could be applied to the pictographs of any language. For more examples of DIP coding see Appendix / Examples DIP.

老子之

道德經

Lao Zi's

Dao De Jing

CHINESE-ENGLISH DICTIONARY

LAO ZI'S DAO DE JING

nemonik-thinking.org

Legend

Line sequence: *Digital Index for Pictographs (DIP)* – simplified pictograph (traditional pictograph) – Pinyin – English meaning.

000000

000000 〇 líng: zero.

001001 儿 (兒) ér: child, male, second, second time, son, stupid, twice, two, youngster.

001100 人 rén: everybody, human being, man, mankind, other people, people, person, person engaged in particular activity, someone else.

001100 人为 rénwéi: artificial, having human cause or origin, human attempt or effort, man-made.

001100 人为德 rénwéidé: artificial virtue.

001100 人之 rénzhī: ability to appreciate a person's character and capability, aid somebody in doing a good job, answer a fool according to his folly, be anxious to help those in need, be eager to help those in danger, breaking all resistance, care for the children of other family as we care for our own, deal with somebody as he deals with you, deceptive talk, do unto them as they do unto us, does somebody, excel in martial arts, give a dose of his own medicine, heaven never cuts off a

nemonik-thinking.org

man's means - there is always a way out, help somebody to fulfil his wish, honour the aged of other family as we honour our own, like entering an unpopulated land, miracle, pay back in his own coin, pay back in kind, profit at other's expense, requite like for like, take advantage of another's perilous state, take advantage of somebody's precarious position, the way of the world, what is natural and normal, with his own physique.

001100 人事 rénshì: consciousness, consciousness of the world, facts of life, human affairs, personal relations, personnel, personnel matters, sexual awareness, sexual passion, ways of the world, what is humanly possible.

001100 人居 rénjū: dwelling, human habitat, man's residence.

001100 人心 rénxīn: conscience, popular feeling, will of the people.

001100 人类 rénlèi: man, mankind, people, someone else.

001100 人之道 rénzhīdào: Confucian way of gentlemen, people's way, way of people.

nemonik-thinking.org

001110 小 xiǎo: concubine, few, for a while, insignificant, little, minor, petty, short time, small, tiny, young, youngest.

001110 小心 xiǎoxīn: careful, take care.

001200 义 (義) yì: friendly feelings, just, justice, meaning, right conduct, righteousness.

001200 入 rù: admitted, agree, become a member, come into, confirm, conform, enlist, enter, income, into, join.

001200 入于 (入於) rùyú: into the, penetrate.

001201 心 xīn: centre, core, heart, intelligence, intention, middle, mind, opinion, soul.

002200 从 (從) cōng, cóng, zōng, zòng: accessory, accomplice, adopt, adopting action or attitude, by, comply, engage, ever - followed by negative - meaning never, follow, follower, from, go in for, join, lax, obey, observe, pass by, passing through, past, regain, related by common paternal grandfather or earlier ancestor, retainer, second cousin, since, submit, taken up with, through - gap, unhurried, via, whence, yielding.

002200 父 fǔ, fù: father.

002200 从事 (從事) cóngshì: deal with, do, engage, go for, handle, undertake.

002201 必 bì: certainly, have to, must, necessarily, surely, will.

003200 公 gōng: collective, collectively owned, common, duke, equitable, fair, father-in-law, general, highest of five orders of nobility, honourable - gentlemen - designation, international - high seas - metric system - calendar, just, make public, male, male animal, official business, public, universally acknowledged.

003201 兆 zhào: augury, betoken, billion, forebode, foreshadow, foretell, manifest, mega, million, omen, predict, presage, sign, tera-, trillion.

003300 众 (眾), 衆 zhòng: crowd, many, many people, masses, multitude, numerous, public.

003300 众人 (眾人, 衆人) zhòngrén: everybody, many people.

003300 众多 (眾多) zhòngduō: numerous.

005000 乡 (鄉) xiāng, xiǎng, xiàng: country, countryside, famous land, home village or town, hometown, native place, rural area, township, village.

011011 也 yě: all, also, as well as, either, even, final particle implying affirmation or identity, is, isn't it, or, pause in speaking - comma - colon - semicolon, too.

nemonik-thinking.org

012001 化 huā, huà: become, change, convert, digest, -ization, -ize, make into, melt, reform misguided person through persuasion, thaw, transform.

012100 介 jiè: armour, between, forerunner, harbinger, herald, interpose, introduce, lie between, mind, preposition, principle, principled, sea shell, serious, shell, situated between, straightforward, to heart, upright, upstanding, wear armour.

012100 少 shǎo, shào: few, inadequate, lack, less, little, lose, missing, moment, rarely, seldom, short off, short while, young.

012100 爪 zhǎo, zhuǎ: animal feet, claw, nail, talon.

012200 以 yǐ: according, at, because, by, by means of, consider, follow order, for, hold, in, in order to, in some place or time, place, purpose, so as to, take, thereby, therefore, to, use, with.

012200 以下 yǐxià: below, the following, under.

012200 以不知 yǐbùzhī: not to claim to know.

012200 以为 (以為) yǐwéi: believe, consider, think, thought, under the impression.

012200 以免 yǐmiǎn: in case, in order to avoid, so as not to.

012200 以此 yǐcǐ: because of this, for this reason, hence, on this account, thereby, thus, with this.

012200 以至 yǐzhì: down to, so, so that, to such an extent that, up to.

012200 以至于 (以至於) yǐzhìyú: down to, even, so that, the extent that, to such an extent, up to.

012200 以降 yǐjiàng: dynasty, since some point in the past.

019002 毳 cuì: brittle, crisp, down, fine hair on animal, fine hair or fur on animals.

021000 川 chuān: area of level country, boil, creek, flow, plain, river, stream.

021000 川谷 (川穀) chuāngǔ: Agrestis, erroneously called Chinese pearl barley, Job's tears - Coix lacryma.

022011 他 tā: another, elsewhere, he, him, it, other, she, used as a meaningless mock object, used before name for emphasis, used for either sex when the sex is unknown or unimportant.

022200 代 dài: act for others, act on behalf of others, age, displace, dynasty, eon - geological, era - historical, generation, geological era, historical period, period, replace, replacement of person or generation, substitute, take the place of.

023200 伐 fá: attack, boast, cut down, cut tree, descend upon, dispatch an expedition against, fell, subjugate.

100000

100000 一 yī: 1, a - article, all, alone, an - article, as soon as, entire, one, same, single, the One, throughout, whole.

100000 一生 yīshēng: a lifetime, all one's life, for life, from the cradle to the grave, in one's life, one's whole life, throughout one's life.

100110 寸 cùn: inch, small, thumb, tiny, unit of length.

101001 九 jiǔ: nine, 9.

101001 九成 jiǔchéng: nine-tenths, ninety percent.

101001 几 (幾) jī, jǐ: achieve, almost, attain, bench, close, dangerous, few, fine, government affairs, how many, how much, insignificant, less, long narrow table, near, nearly, omen, reach, several, slight, small, small table, some, symptom of a trend, what.

101001 几何 (幾何) jǐhé: geometry, how many, how much.

101010 力 lì: ability, capability, force, influence power, power, strength, strenuously.

101010 才 (纔) cái: ability, capable individual, endowment, expert, gift, just now, moment ago, not until, only, only after, only if, only then, really, somebody of a certain type, talent.

101100 丈 zhàng: brother in law, elder person, father in law, gentleman, husband, man, measure land, old man, support with the hand, ten feet, unit of length - 3.3 meters.

101100 又 yòu: add, again, also, and, and then, another, both, but, even, in addition, predict, too, used to stress, what's more.

101100 大 dà, dài, tài: big, big way, deep, doctor, eldest, fully, grandeur, great, greatly, high, huge, large, large scale, major, more than half, most, oldest, vast, wide.

101100 大丈夫 dàizhàngfu, dàzhàngfu, dàzhàngfū: accomplishment, ambition, gentleman, great man, man of ambition and achievement, man of character or real worth, man with aspiration, real man.

101100 大事 dàshì: do something in a big way, greatly, important event, major event, major political event - war or change of regime, major social event - wedding or funeral.

101100 大于 (大於) dàyú: bigger than, greater than.

nemonik-thinking.org

101100 大人 dàren: adult, grownup, title of respect toward superiors.

101100 大作 dàzuò: exaggerate, make something big of it, masterpiece, sudden big and impressive event - sound - flash - burst – wind.

101100 大器 dàqì: great talent, one of outstanding talents, treasure.

101100 大器晚成 dàqìwǎnchéng: great talent takes time to develop, in the fullness of time a major figure will develop into a pillar of the state, it takes a long time to make a big pot - idiom, Rome wasn't built in a day.

101100 大国 (大國) dàguó: great power, leading powers, power, power - i.e. a dominant country.

101100 大小 dàxiǎo: adults and children, anyway, consideration of seniority, dimension, large and small, magnitude, measurement, people, seniority, size, total.

101100 大方 dàfāng: easy-mannered, expert, generous, green tea, in good taste, magnanimous, mother earth, natural and relaxed, potent prescription, scholar, stylish.

101100 大笑 dàxiào: belly laugh, laugh heartily, laughter.

101100 大象 dàxiàng: elephant.

101100 大道 dàdào: avenue, main road, main street, the Great Way – Tao.

101100 广 (廣) ān, guǎng, yǎn: broad, expand, extensive, numerous, spread, vast, wide.

101101 凡 fán: all, altogether, any, approximation, common, commonplace, every, gist, material world as opposed to supernatural or immortal levels, mortal world, mundane, note on musical scale, ordinary, outline, temporal, whatever, worldly.

101101 尤 yóu: against, discontentment, especially, express, fail, fault, mistake, outstanding, particularly, worry.

101110 习 (習) xí: custom, flapping wings, habit, practise, study, used

101111 仓 (倉) cāng: barn, berth, cabin, granary, hold - ship, sea, store, storehouse.

101200 之 zhī: 's, go to, her, him, his, it, its, marks preceding phrase as modifier of following phrase, possessive particle - him, their, them.

101200 之上 zhīshàng: above, over.

101200 之下 zhīxià: beneath, less than, under.

101200 之前 zhīqián: ago, before, beforehand, previously, prior to.

101200 之后 (之後) zhīhòu: after, afterwards, following, later.

101200 之物 zhīwù: external things, mere worldly possessions, thing.

101200 之至 zhīzhì: extremely, greatly, most, very much.

101200 之间 (之間) zhījiān: among, between, inter.

101200 六 liù, lù: six, 6.

101200 六亲 (六親) liùqīn: family relationships, one's kin, six close relatives - father - mother - older brothers - younger brothers - wife - male children.

101200 太 tài: big, excessively, extreme, great, highest, much, senior, so, superior - above, that, too, very.

101200 文 wén, wèn: achievements in culture and education, appearance, article, articles of decree, character, civilian, civilian post, classics, coins, composition, cover up, culture, decorate, disordered, document, embroidered, essay, figure, fine, form, formal, gentle, good, gorgeous, humanities, language, literally, literary, literary language, literary talent, literature, magnificent, mental labour, mild, music, natural phenomenon, record, rites, script, slogan, study diligently, tattoo - skin, tune, veins, verse, virtue, write, writing, written language.

101200 文彩 wéncǎi: iridescent.

101200 文采 wéncǎi: flowery language, literary grace, literary talent, rich and bright colours.

101200 犬 quán: dog.

101210 为 (為, 爲) wéi, wèi: act, action, am, are, as - in the capacity of, be, because, become, been, behave as, being, do, for, govern, handle, interfere, is, practise, pursue, serve as, take something as, take...to be, to, was, were.

101210 为主 (為主) wéizhǔ: attach most importance to, based, first impressions are strongest, give first place to, give priority to, rely mainly on, reverse the positions of the host and the guest, turn from a guest into a host.

101210 为此 (為此) wèicǐ: for this purpose, for this reason, in order to do this, in this connection, in this respect, therefore, to this end, with regards to this.

101301 忒 tè, tēi: change, changeable, err, error, excessive, mistake, too, very-usually of objectionable things.

102010 刃 rèn: blade, cutlery, edge of blade, edged tool, knife, knife edge, sword.

102011 孔 kǒng: aperture, cave dwellings, great, hole, opening, orifice.

102100 久 jiǔ: always, continue, endure, for a long time, forever, grow late, last long, long duration of time, long time, permanent, time passage.

102100 夕 xī, xì: dusk, evening, night, slanted, sunset.

102101 庀 pǐ: administer, arrange, prepare, provide, regulate to hand up.

102101 龙 (龍) lóng, lǒng, máng: dragon, fine horse, imperial, not round, outstanding person, symbolic of emperor, upright, vigorous.

102110 乎 hū, hú: final particle - expressing question or doubt.

102110 分 fēn, fèn: 0.01 yuan - unit of money, allocate, assign, branch, distinguish, distinguish - good and bad, divide, fraction, minute - time, one tenth - of certain units, part or subdivision, percent, point in sports or games, separate, unit of length of 3 mm.

102110 水 shuǐ: additional charges or income, beverage, juice, liquid, lotion, number of washes of clothes, river, water.

102200 今 jīn: current, modern era, now, present-day, this, today.

102210 亦 yì: also, as well as, likewise, too.

102210 杀 (殺) sà, shā, shài, shè: check, counteract, curtail, execute, extremely - after verb, fight, hurt, kill, murder, reduce, slaughter, slay, smart, weaken.

102210 杀人 (殺人) shārén: homicide, kill a person, murder.

102300 交 jiāo: arrive, associate, boundary, communicate, cross, deliver, entrust, exchange, friendship, hand in, hand over, intersect, intersect, make friends, mix, pay money, reach, turn over, unite.

102300 交际 jiāojì: communication, social intercourse.

102300 令 líng, lǐng, lìng: allow, cause, command, commandant, decree, demand, drinking game, excellent, give a name, good, government position, honorific title, honourable, if, laws, let, lucky, magistrate, make, make something happen, obey, official title, order, ream of paper, renown, reputation, season, song-poem, virtuous, wagtail, warrant, writ, your.

102300 令人 lìngrén: cause somebody to do, make one do something - e.g. ponder, make one feel something, used in constructing words for feelings such as anger - surprise - sympathy etc..

102300 兴 (興) xīng, xìng: allow, become, begin, desire, encourage, excitement, fashion to, feeling, flourish, get up, interest, maybe, permit, popular, prevail, promote, prosper, rise, start, thrive.

102300 冬 (鼕) dōng: drumming, knock, rat-a-tat, rub-a-dub, sound of beating a drum, winter.

102310 求 qiú: beg, beseech, demand, entreat, look for, request, seek, strive, try to obtain.

102310 求得 qiúdé: ask for something and receive it, look for and obtain, obtained, try to obtain.

102310 求生 qiúshēng: possess the will to live, seek survival, seek to live on.

103010 勿 wù: do not, must not, never do not, not, without.

103011 托 (託) tuō: asked to take care, base, commit, entrust, excuse, give, hold in one's hand, hold on the palm of hand, hold up with palm, prop, rely on, rest - arm rest, set, support, support for weight, support in one's palm, thanks to, trust, trustee, used to support something.

103100 反 fǎn: against, analogy, anti-, betray, contrary, give back, go or come back, in reverse, inside-out or upside-down, instead, inverse, launch counter-attack, on the contrary, oppose, opposite, otherwise, rebel, reciprocate, resist, return, reverse, strike back, turn back, turn over, wrong side out or up.

103100 反物质 fǎnwùzhì: antimatter.

103100 灭 (滅) miè: drown, exterminate, extinguish -fire, go out - fire, kill, put out - fire, submerge, wipe out.

103101 它 tā, tuō: it.

103110 乐 (樂) lè, liáo, luò, yào, yuè: cheerful, delighted, enjoy, enjoyable, glad, happy, laugh, like, music, pleasure.

103111 犹 (猶) yóu: as, as if, grand plan, hesitant, just as, just like, like, monkey, shilly-shally, similar, son of dog, still, still - undecided, too, uncertain, yet.

103120 孙 (孫) sūn, xùn: descendant, grandchild, grandson, three generations.

nemonik-thinking.org

104200 玄 xuán, xuàn: abstruse, black, deep, fantastic, mysterious, mystery, profound, unbelievable.

104200 玄之又玄 xuánzhīyòuxuá: abstruse, explaining what is unknown by what is still more unknown, extremely mysterious, hard to comprehend, most mysterious of the mysterious, mysteries of the Dao according to Laozi, mystery of mysteries, mystery within a mystery, profound and mysterious.

104200 玄牝 xuánpìn: mysterious female.

104211 忽 hū: abruptly, ignore, inattention, measure unit, neglect, now, occasionally, overlook, suddenly.

105110 幼 yào, yòu: child, immature, infant, under age, young, young child.

105500 爽 shuāng, shuǎng: bright, cheerful, clear, crisp, deviate, feel well, fine, frank, happy, invigorating, open, openhearted, pleasurable, refresh, refreshing, straightforward, well.

106110 约 (約) yāo, yuē: about, agreement, appointment, approximately, around, arrange, ask, bind, brief, covenant, economical, frugal, indistinct, invite, make appointment, pact, reduce, restrain, restrict, simple, treaty, weigh, weigh in a balance or on a scale.

106200 炊 chuī: cook food, dress food, meal, steam.

107110 纷 (紛) fēn: confused, disarrange, disaster, disorder, dispute, horsetail bag, lace, many, numerous, rag, ribbon on a flag, scattered, tangled, various.

107300 终 (終) zhōng: all, die, end, finally, finish, in the end.

107300 终于 (終於) zhōngyú: at last, at long last, eventually, finally, in the end.

107300 终日 (終日) zhōngrì: all day long, whole day.

107300 终朝 zhōngzhāo, zhōngcháo: all day, all morning, towards the end, whole morning.

107300 终身 (終身) zhōngshēn: all one's life, lifelong, marriage, one's whole life.

107400 奚 xī, xí: how, servant, what, where, why.

107400 淡 dàn, tán, yǎn, yàn: bland, diluted, feint, fresh, indifferent, insipid, light in colour, meaningless, mild, nitrogen, not salty, pale, slack, tasteless, thin, trivial, watery, weak.

107410 紛: Mentioned in some versions, but replaced with the simplified 107110 纷.

109300 兹 (茲) cí, zī: at this time, dirty, grow, here, hereby, herewith, muddy, now, presently, this, time, year.

nemonik-thinking.org

109501 慈 cí: amiable, benevolent, charitable, charitable, compassion, gentle, humane, kind, loving, merciful

110000 十 shí: 10, complete, perfect, ten, tenth.

110000 十百 shíbǎi: thousand.

110100 下 xià: below, bottom, bring down, decline, down, downwards, fall, finish, give, go down, inferior, issue, later, latter under, lay egg, low, lower, lower level, lower position, next - week, next time, put in, second of two parts, servant, subject - servant, under, underneath.

110100 下流 xiàliú: dirty, dirty jokes, low-class, lower part river, mean and lowly, obscene, vulgar.

110110 门 (門) mén: access, branch of study, branches of technology, category, class, door, doorway, entrance, exit, family, gate, gateway, home, house, knack, large guns, lessons, method, opening, phylum or division - taxonomy, religious sect, school of thought, sect, subjects, switch, valve, way, way to do something.

111000 千 (韆) qiān: great amount, great number, many, numerous, swindler, swing, thousand, very.

111000 千里 qiānlǐ: far away, long distance, thousand li - i.e. 500 kilometres, thousand miles.

111100 不 bù: cannot, do not, negative prefix when directly preceding a tone, no, not, un-.

111100 不为 (不為) bùwéi: do all manner of evil, not, not to be repeated, not to be taken as a precedent, stop at nothing, what is there against it, why not go ahead with it.

111100 不争 (不爭) bùzhēng: beyond doubt, incontestable, not contend, not strive, unarguable, unassailable, undeniable, undoubted, widely known.

111100 不仁 bùrén: heartless, not benevolent, numb.

111100 不信 bùxìn: distrust, See 不 not & 信 trust = distrust.

111100 不克 bùkè: cannot, impossible, not be able, unable.

111100 不单 (不單) bùdān: not merely, not simply, not the only.

111100 不厌 (不厭) bùyàn: not mind doing something, not object, not tire of.

111100 不可 bùkě: cannot, forbidden, must not, not allowed, should not.

111100 不可以 bùkěyǐ: cannot, may not, not, not be, should not.

111100 不和 bùhé: at odds, discord, disharmonious, not get along well, on bad terms.

111100 不善 bùshàn: bad, ill, incompetent, not as good, not good, not good at, not to be pooh-poohed, quite impressive, See 不 not & 善 competent, unkind.

111100 不如 bùrú: inferior to, it would be better to, not as good as, not equal to.

111100 不屈 bùqū: not yield, unbending, unyielding.

111100 不得 bùdé: cannot, may not, must not, not allowed, not supposed, should not.

111100 不得已 bùdéyǐ: act against one's will, have no alternative, have no choice, have to, must.

111100 不怠 bùdài: indefatigable, not relent, sedulous, untiring, work hard.

111100 不成 bùchéng: can that be - at the end of a rhetorical question, insufficient, not enough, unable, won't do, would not do.

111100 不敢 bùgǎn: not dare.

111100 不敢为天下先 bùgǎnwéitiānxiàxiān: not daring to act as the world's first, humble, humility.

111100 不明 bùmíng: fail to understand, missing, not clear, unknown.

nemonik-thinking.org

111100 不智 bùzhì: unwise.

111100 不欲 (不慾) bùyù: anorexia, do not war t to, grieve to the extent of wishing to die.

111100 不死 bùsǐ: immortal, See 不 not & 死 die = immortal.

111100 不殆 bùdài: never-losing, not be threatened, without danger.

111100 不治 bùzhì: anarchy, dead, die of illness or injury despite medical help, incurable, ungoverned

111100 不满 (不滿) bùmǎn: discontented, dissatisfied, resentful.

111100 不然 bùrán: different, if not, no, not so, or else, otherwise.

111100 不用 bùyòng: disuse, need not, nonutility.

111100 不畏 bùwèi: challenge, defy, difficulties, not fear, not to be afraid of difficulties, scorn, unafraid.

111100 不知 bùzhī: beyond somebody, ignorant, in the dark, it beats me, know nothing about, last person to know, no clue, no idea, not aware, not know, not to admit - defeat - hardships - tiredness etc., nct to hear about, not to know, unaware, unknowingly, without knowledge.

111100 不祥 bùxiáng: ill omen, inauspicious, misfortune, ominous, unlucky.

111100 不穷 (不窮) bùqióng: appear frequently, boundless, emerge one after another, endless, inexhaustible, too numerous to be counted.

111100 不笑 bùxiào: do not laugh, put on a false smile.

111100 不绝 (不絕) bùjué: endless, unending, uninterrupted.

111100 不肖 bùxiào: different, not similar, unfilial, unworthy, worthless fellow.

111100 不胜 (不勝) bùshèng: cannot bear or stand, deeply, extremely, unequal, very.

111100 不能 bùnéng: cannot, must not, should not, unable.

111100 不自 bùzì: ask for trouble, not self-, unbearably sad.

111100 不若 bùruò: inferior, not as, not as good as, not equal to, not if.

111100 不行 bùxíng: awfully, deeply, extremely, insufficient, no good, not allowed, not capable, not enough, not good, not satisfactory, not up to standard, not work, out of the question, poor, won't do, would not do.

111100 不见 (不見) bùjiàn: disappeared, have not seen, missing, not meeting, not seeing.

111100 不足 bùzú: beneath, beneath discussion, cannot, deficiency, inadequate, insufficient, lack, less than, not deserve, not enough, not worth, not worth mentioning, shortage, should not.

111100 不辍 (不輟) bùchuò: ceaseless, forever, incessant, not stop, relentless, stopped working.

111100 不过 (不過) bùguò: anyway - to get back to a previous topic, but, except that, however, merely, no more than, only.

111100 木 mù: coffin, leaf, lumber, musical instruments, numb, simple, stupid, timber, tree, wood, wooden ware.

111201 礼 (禮) lǐ: ceremony, courtesy, ethics, etiquette, formalism, gift, manners, present, propriety, rites, salute, social custom.

111311 闷 (悶) mēn, mèn: airtight, bored, close, cover tightly, depressed, dull sound, gloomy, keep silent, low spirits, melancholy, muffled, sad, sealed, shut indoors, shut oneself in, silent, smother, stop speaking, stuffy, suffocate, tightly closed, tongue-tied, vexed.

111311 闷闷 (悶悶) mènmèn: in low spirits, very depressed.

112000 斤 jīn: axe, catty - approximately 500 g, chopper, keen, shrewd, unit of weight - 500 grams.

112001 比 bǐ, bì, pí, pǐ: associate, compare, compete, contrast, copy, draw a parallel, follow, for example, gesture with hands, liken, near, particle used for comparison - and - "-er than", ratio, such as, than, to.

112100 长 (長) cháng, zhǎng, zhàng: acquire, always, begin to grow, chief, come into being, constantly, develop, elder, elder brother, endure, enhance, escalate, excel, forever, forms - grow, forte, grow, head - teacher, increase, leader, length, long, older, senior, strong point.

112100 长久 (長久) chángjiǔ: for a long time, long-term.

112100 长生 (長生) chángshēng: immortal, live forever, long life, longevity.

112100 长短 (長短) chángduǎn: accident, duration, good and bad, length, long and short, right and wrong.

nemonik-thinking.org

112101 光 guāng: bare, benefit, bright, brilliant, glare, glint, glorify, just, light, merely, only, ray, scenery, shine, smooth, use up.

112200 伏 fú: admit, bend over, conceal - ambush, concede defeat, crawl, crouch, fall - go down, go down, hide - ambush, hottest days of summer, lean over, lie hidden, lie low, overcome, prostrate, subdue, submit, subside, volt.

112200 处 (處) chǔ, chù: are, be in, be situated at, bureau, certain condition, deal with, department, discipline, dwell, exist, get along, get on with, handle, in a position, items of damage, live, location, manage, occupy, office, part, penalize, place, point, position, profit, punish, reside, respect, sentence, site, situated in, spot, stay.

112200 外 wài: external, foreign, in addition, other place then were one is, out, outside, outward.

112200 风 (風) fēng, fěng, fèng: air, atmosphere, custom, information, manners, news, scene, style, trend, wind.

112200 齐 (齊) jī, jì, jiǎn, qí, zhāi, zī: all together, at the same time, even, identical, join, level with, make even, neat, reach, ready, simultaneous.

nemonik-thinking.org

112201 忧 (憂) yōu: anxiety, anxious, concern, grief, grieved, inconvenienced by being orphaned, melancholy, parent's funeral, sad, sorrow, sorrowful, worried.

112210 伪 (偽, 僞) wěi, wèi: bogus, cheat, counterfeit, disguise, do, fake, false, feign, forge, hypocrisy, illegal, pretend, puppet, sham, swindle, unlawful.

112210 网 (網) wǎng: fabric, final result, net, nett capital, network.

112300 状 (狀) zhuàng: accusation, appearance, condition, form, great, lawsuit, legal case, official, shape, shaped, state, state of affairs, strong, suit.

112300 议 (議) yì: comment, consult, criticize, discuss, opinion, propose, suggest, talk over.

113001 牝 pìn: deep gorge, female, female of species, keyhole, mother, valley.

113001 牝牡 pìnmǔ: male and female, superficiality.

113010 仞 rèn: fathom, unit of measure - 8 feet, fathom – measure.

113100 乔 (喬) qiáo: arrogance, assuming, disguise, high mountain, lofty, pride, proud, stately, tall.

nemonik-thinking.org

113200 衣 yī, yì: afterbirth, clothes, clothing, cover, dress, gown, put on clothes, skin, wear.

113210 我 wǒ: I, me, my, our, ourselves, us, we

113300 采 (採) cǎi, cài: affairs, allotment to a noble, choose, collect, extract, gather, mine, pick, p uck, select.

113310 剑 (劍) jiàn: blows of sword, dagger, double-edged sword, sabre, sword.

114110 你 nǐ: second person pronoun you.

114200 妙 miào: clever, excellent, exquisite, extraordinary, fine, ingenious, mystery, subtle, wonder, wonderful.

114200 私 sī: illegal, illicit, personal, private, secret, selfish.

114201 垗 zhào: burial ground, cemetery, grave yard, place inside the altar wall, sacrifice.

114210 孤 gū: fatherless, isolated, lonely, orphan, solitary.

114210 孤寡 gūguǎ: lonely, orphans and widows.

114400 浅 (淺) jiān, qiǎn: carry out, easy, fulfil, l ght - of colour, loose, narrow, not close, not deep, not intimate, not long in time, shallow, simple, sound of moving water, superficial.

115200 恢 huī: big, extensive, great, high, immense, recover, restore, vast.

115200 恢恢 huīhuī: extensive - literary, vast.

115311 惚 bū, hū: absent-minded, confused, dim, faint, indistinct, trance.

116300 彩 (綵) cǎi: applause, bright - colour, colour, coloured silk, hue, prize - lottery, splendour, variegated colours, variety.

117300 谈 (談) tán: chat, conversation, converse, discuss, speak, surname, talk.

119500 飚 (飈) biāo: stormy gale, whirlwind, wind, alternative 飙 41580.

121000 什 (甚) shén, shèn, shí: abandon oneself, any, assorted, blame, certainly, considerably, deep, dote on spouse, even, extremely, file of ten soldiers, formidable, great, great extent, important, indulge, make a pet of spouse, miscellaneous, mixed, more than, most, one-hundred per cent, overdo, prevailing, really, serious, ten - tenfold - one tenth, tenfold, terrible, too far, varied, very, what, why, writings.

121000 什伯 shénbǎi: thousand.

121000 卅 sà: 30, thirty, thirtieth.

121001 见 (見) jiàn, xiàn: appear, behold, catch sight, contact, display, expose, insight, interview, look, meet, observe, perceive, refer, see, show, understand, view.

121010 币 (幣) bì: belongings, coin, currency, dilapidated, legal tender, money, old, present, property, shabby, silk, worn-out.

121100 业 (業) yè: achievement, already, board, business, cause, course of study, engage, enterprise, estate, industry, job, line of business, occupation, profession, property, study, trade, work.

121100 凶 (兇) xiōng: bad, culprit, famine, fearful, ferocious, fierce, inauspicious, misfortune, murder, ominous, sad, terrible, terrible, vicious.

121100 凶事 xiōngshì: fateful accident, inauspicious matter involving death or casualties, unlucky matters - death - burial, violence that involves casualties, war.

121100 凶年 (兇年) xiōngnián: bad year, famine year, off year, year of famine.

121120 刚 (剛) gāng: barely, exactly, firm, hard, just, rigid, staunch, strong, tough.

121120 刚强 (剛強) gāngqiáng: firm, unyielding.

nemonik.thinking.org

121200 朴 (樸) piáo, pō, pò, pú, pǔ: Celtis sinensis var. japonica, honest, plain, pure, simple, sincere, tree, unadorned.

122001 华 (華) huā, huá, huà: abbreviation for China, brilliance, Chinese, extravagant, flowery, fruitless flower, gorgeous, halo, illustrious, luxurious, magnificent, splendid, splendour.

122001 此 cǐ: choose, from now on, here, his, in this case, now, position, right now, then, these, this, those.

122001 此道 cǐdào: such matters, things like this, this endeavour, this hobby, this line of work, this pursuit, this road.

122011 地 de, dì: background, earth, farmland, field, floor, ground, instance, land, linking it to preceding modifying adverbial adjunct, location, -ly, particle used before a verb or adjective, place, realm, region, soil, the Earth.

122110 利 lì: advantage, beneficial, do good, favourable, gains, interest, merit, profit, sharp.

122110 利剑 (利劍) lìjiàn: sharp sword.

122110 利器 lìqì: able individual, effective implement, sharp weapon, useful tool.

122200 怀 (懷) huái: become pregnant, bosom, breast, carry, carry in bosom, cherish, conceive a ch ld, heart, keep in mind, mind, think of, yearn.

122200 氐 dǐ: arrive, base, foundation, on the whole, reach, root of tree.

122300 怵 chù: afraid, fear, feel deeply about, lament over, shy, timid.

122300 怵怵 chùchù: See 怵 timid, very timid.

122300 补 (補) bǔ: fill, fill - vacancy, fix, make up for, mend, nourish, patch, repair, restore, supplement, supply.

123100 攸 yōu: adverbial prefix, contended, distant, far, fleeting, flowing, self-satisfied.

123201 恍 huǎng: absent minded, alike, as if, be like, blurred, dimly, disappointed, disquieted, elusive, faintly, fleet, flurried, indistinct, mad, more or less the same, seem, sudden, trance.

123210 剉: Mentioned in some versions, but replaced with the simplified 524200 锉.

124301 悠 yōu: leisure, remote, swing, at ease, distant, far, leisurely, long, long in time, long or drawn out, pensive, remote, remote in time or space, sad, swing, worried.

125010 彻 (徹) chè: tax duties (ancient), clear, complete, dismantle, finish, leak, pass through, penetrate, pervade, pierce, reclaim, remove, sufficient, thorough-going, understand.

126100 修 xiū: accomplish, build, cultivate, cultivate to decorate, decorate, edit, embellish, mend, prune, repair, self-cultivation, study, training, trim, write.

131100 仚 xiān: fly.

131110 则 (則) zé: be, but, conjunction expressing contrast with a previous sentence or clause, contrast, follow, get near, grades, imitate, in that case, law, nearby, norm, official statement, principle, regulation, rule, so that, standard, then, when, while, will, written items.

132100 芥 gài, jiè: chock, Indian mustard, knot, minor matter, mustard, mustard plant, petty thing, see, small grass, tiny, trifle.

133101 货 (貨) huò: commodities, goods, money, products.

134100 依 yī, yǐ: according, agree, based on, comply, consent, count on, depend, forgive, in the light of, judging, lean against, listen, listen - comply, near, obey a wish, rely on, set in, tolerant.

134300 贱 (賤) jiàn: base, cheap, contemptible, despicable, humble, ignoble, inexpensive, low, low rank, low-down, lowly, low-priced, mean, my, worthless.

136300 峻 jùn: harsh, high, high mountains, severe, steep, stern, towering.

138200 幽 yōu: dark, dim, hidden, hidden away, imprison, peaceful, quiet, remote, secluded, serene, tranquil, underworld.

143300 贷 (貸) dài, tè: borrow, forgive, give, lend, leniency, loan, make excuses, pardon, shift responsibility, shirk, take out a loan

200000

200000 二 èr: 2, second time, second, stupid, twice, two.

200010 于 (於) xū, yú: as, at, by, for, from, go, in, on, out of, sentence-final interrogative particle, take, than, to.

201001 元 yuán: chief, coin, component, dollar, dynasty, first, fundamental, head, origin, primary.

201001 无 (無) mó, wú: empty, have no empty, have not, lack, -less, negative, no, no matter, non-being, none,

nemonik-thinking.org

Non-existence, not, not have, opposite of 有 existence, regardless, there is not, un-, what is not, without.

201001 无不 (無不) wúbù: all, all without exception, all-conquering, do not care one way or another, ever victorious, everyone without exception, everything is there, indifferent, invariable, invincible, none lacking, none missing, say all you know and say it without reserve, win in every battle.

201001 无为 (無為) wúwéi: Daoist doctrine of inaction, inaction, inactivity, laissez-faire, let things take their own course, Non-action, non-interference.

201001 无争 (無爭) wúzhēng: bear no ill will against anybody.

201001 无以 wúyǐ: difficult, unable.

201001 无关 (無關) wúguān: independence, irrelevant, no relationship or connection with, nothing to do with, unconcerned, unrelated.

201001 无厌 (無厭) wúyàn: insatiable.

201001 无名 (無名) wúmíng: anonymous, nameless, no name, obscure, unknown.

201001 无味 (無味) wúwèi: insipid, odourless, tasteless, unpalatable.

201001 无常 (無常) wúcháng: changeable, die, fickle, ghost taking away the soul after death, impermanence, pass away, transiency, variable.

201001 无形 (無形) wúxíng: formless, imperceptible, incorporeal, intangible, invisible, invisible assets, virtual.

201001 无心 (無心) wúxīn: inadvertently, not in the mood, not intentionally, unintentionally, unwittingly.

201001 无恒 (無恆) wúhéng: inconsistent, inconstant, lack patience, lacking in perseverance.

201001 无情 (無情) wúqíng: heartless, inexorable, merciless, pitiless, ruthless.

201001 无敌 (無敵) wúdí: invincible, paragon, unconquerable, unequalled, unmatched, without rival.

201001 无有 wúyòu: Non-existence.

201001 无极 (無極) wújí: electrodeless, moderate, non-polar.

201001 无正 wúzhèng: abnormal, not normal, strange.

201001 无物 (無物) wúwù: devoid of content, have nothing, nothing.

201001 无状 (無狀) wúzhuàng: ill-mannered, insolent, no shape, no state, shapeless.

nemonik-thinking.org

201001 无瑕 (無瑕) wúxiá: faultless, flawless, perfect, without blemish.

201001 无知 (無知) wúzhī: ignorance.

201001 无私 (無私) wúsī: altruistic, disinterested, self-forgetful, selfless, unselfish.

201001 无能 (無能) wúnéng: inability, incapable, incompetent, inefficient, powerless, without talent.

201001 无道 (無道) wúdào: brutal regime, injustice, tyranny.

201001 无间 (無間) wújiàn: continuously, hard to separate, indistinguishable, make no distinction, no gap between them, not keeping anything from each other, unbroken, very close, very close to each other, without interruption.

201010 万 (萬) mò, wàn: absolutely, all, by all means, extreme, great number, many, much, myriad, ten thousand, great number, many, much, innumerable, ten thousand.

201010 万有引力 wànyǒuyǐnlì: gravity.

201010 万物 (萬物) wànwù: all living things, all things on earth, creation.

201010 子 zi, zǐ: 11th solar month, 1st earthly branch, 1st terrestrial branch, adopt as son, affiliated, although, baby, bear fruit, chess piece, child, coin, daughter, descendants, egg, fourth of five orders of nobility, fruit, honorific title with the surname, infant, literate and officialdom, love, man, master, midnight, noun suffix, offspring, only, person, seed, serve one's parents with filial devotion, small, something small and hard, son, sub-, subsidiary, tender, though, viscount, year of the rat, you, young.

201010 子孙 (子孫) zǐsūn: children, descendants, grandchildren, offspring, posterity.

201010 手 shǒu: convenient, expert, hand, hold, person engaged in certain types of work, personal, skilled person.

201100 天 tiān: before dawn, celestial, day, god, heaven, nature, overhead - above, season, sky, time, timing, weather.

201100 天下 tiānxià: country, domination, land under heaven, realm, rule, ruling power, sky under, state, state power, whole world, world.

nemonik-thinking.org

201100 天之道 tiānzhīdào: nature's way, way of nature - ambiguous because it could refer to heaven.

201100 天地 tiāndì: field - science, field of activity, heavens and earth, scope, sky and earth, universe, world.

201100 天堂 tiāntáng: heaven or paradise.

201100 天大 tiāndà: as big as the sky, as large as the heavens, enormous, extremely big, gargantuan.

201100 天子 tiānzǐ: Emperor, rightful emperor, Son of Heaven.

201100 天道 tiāndào: good or ill omen, heavenly law, manifestation of God's will, natural law, weather.

201100 天长地久 (天長地久) tiānchángdìjiǔ: enduring while the world lasts - idiom, eternal.

201100 夫 fū, fú: begin sentence, conscripted labourer, exclamation mark, form word, grammar particle or demonstrative pronoun, grammar similar to do, he, husband, male adult, man, manual worker, porter, she, that, them, these, they, this, those.

201110 示 qī, shí, shì, zhì: demonstrate, manifest, reveal, show.

nemonik-thinking.org

201200 立 lì, wèi: adopt, appoint, ascend throne, at once, conclude, contribution, draw up, erect, establish, exist, found, immediately, lay down, let stand, live, right away, set, set up, set upright, sign, stand, stand up, upright, vertical, wardrobe.

201210 夺 (奪) duó: compete, force one's way through, leave out, lose, rob, seize, snatch, strive for, take by force, win, wrest control.

201211 氾 fán, fàn, fěng: ancient place, extensive, float, flood, inundate, low, overflow.

202010 乃 (是) nǎi: after all, as it turned out, be, hence, indeed, namely be, only, really, so, then, therefore, thereupon, thus, you, your.

202010 乃至 nǎizhì: even, go so far as to.

202100 云 (雲) yún: cloud, say, saying, speak.

202100 云云 yúnyún: and so, and so forth, and so on, going around, implying that some words of the same purport are left unquoted, like this, many, many and confused, numerous, quotation, revolving, so and so, thus, used at the end of a direct or indirect.

202100 友 yǒu: companion, fraternity, friend.

nemonik-thinking.org

202100 失 shī: break, deviate, fail, fail to attain, fail to keep, fail to live up to, get lost, lose, loss, make mistake, miss, neglect to lose.

202100 失道 shīdào: lose the way, moral failing, unjust cause, unjust cause finds scant support.

202100 矢 shǐ: arrow, dart, swear, vow.

202110 予 yú, yǔ: bestow, give, give grant, giving, I, I - used by emperor, me, praise, sell, surplus.

202110 兮 xī: exclamatory particle, how, part.

202110 宁 (寧) níng, nìng, zhù: calm, healthy, peaceful, prefer, quiet, rather, serene, tranquil.

202200 产 chǎn: estate, give birth, produce, product, property, reproduce, resource.

202200 关 (關) guān, wān: close, concern, custom, frontier pass, imprison, involve, joint, mountain pass, pass, relation, shut, turn off.

202200 厌 (厭) yā, yān, yàn: annoyed, detest, dislike, fed up, loathe, reject, satiate, satisfied, tired of.

202210 余 (餘) yú: after, apart from, endless, extra, full, have eaten one's fill, I, I - used by emperor, infinite, leave, leftover, leisurely, me, more than, my, odd, other, over, plenty, remain, remainder after division, residue - math., second, spare, spare time, surplus.

202210 守 shǒu, shòu: abide by the law, adjoining, conserve, defend, follow, guard, guide, keep watch, look after, nearby, nurse, observe rules or ritual, protect, stand by.

202210 守则 (守則) shǒuzé: regulation, rules.

202210 舟 zhōu: boat, ship.

202300 应 (應) yīng, yìng: accept, agree, answer, comply, cope, correspond, deal, echo, handle, must, ought, promise, respond, should.

202301 汎 fàn, fěng: afloat, broad, careless, drift, float, vast.

203100 及 jí: and, as good as, attain, come up, extend, if, in time, reach, since, up to, when.

203100 及其 jíqí: and, as well as.

203101 死 sǐ: dead, death, die, exceedingly, extremely, fixed, impassable, inflexible, inflexible, rather die than, rigid, stop up, uncrossable.

203101 死者 sǐzhě: dead, deceased, defunct, departed.

203200 会 (會) guì, huì, kuài: able, accounting, assemble, association, balance an account, can, city, fair, gather, group, likely, meet, moment, opportunity, possible, see, sure, understand, union, will.

203200 发 (發, 髮) fā, fà: become, begin, burst, cause to, come into existence, deliver, develop, diffuse, discharge, discover, dispatch, disperse, distribute, emit, exhibit, expand, expose, express, feel, flourish, generate, give out, gunshots -rounds, hair, issue, launch, open up, produce, reach certain state, rise -fermented, send out, set out, shoot, show feelings, spread out, start, turn, utter.

203200 发狂 (發狂) fākuáng: crazy, lose one's senses, mad, out of one's mind, overexcited.

203210 冰 bīng, níng: cool, freezing, ice, ice-cold, methamphetamine.

203312 怨 yuàn: blame, complain, enmity, hatred, resentment.

203400 实 (實) shí: definitely, fact, fill up, fruit, honest, real, reality, really, result, seed, sincere, solid, true.

203400 泛 fá, fán, fàn, fěng: capsize, careless, drift, emerge, emit upwards, extensive, fill the air, float, flood, general, non-specific, overturn, pan- - prefix, reckless, spread, suffuse, suffused with, superficial, topple, vague.

204200 多 duō: for the most part, lot of, many, more, more than, most, much, multi-, numerous, over.

204200 多少 duōshǎo: amount, as much as, how many, how much, more or less, number, somewhat, to some extent, which – number.

204200 多言 duōyán: logo mania, much to say, talkative, wordy.

204200 多闻 (多聞) duōwén: learned, well informed.

204200 妖 yāo: abnormal thing or phenomena, beauty, bewitching, coquettish, demon, devil, enchanting, evil, evil spirit, goblin, gorgeous, monster, ominous, phantom, seductively charming, strange, supernatural, weird, wicked, witch, witchcraft.

204200 次 cì: events, hypo- chemistry, inferior, nfra-, next, n[th], number of times, order, ranking, second, secondary, sequence, sub-, substandard, time, vice-.

204200 矣 xián, yǐ: already, exclamation, final particle at end of sentence - full stop, particle of completed action.

204201 宠 (寵) chǒng: concubine, favour, favourite, love, pamper, spoil, treat with endue care and affection.

nemonik-thinking.org

204210 沕 mì, wù: abstruse, conceal, content, deep, disappear, hide, matter, outside world, produce, profound, property, thing.

204210 狭 (狹) xiá: limit, narrow, narrow-minded.

204210 穷 (窮) qióng: destitute, exhausted, hard pressed, impoverished, poor, pushed to limit.

204401 怒 nù: angry, flourishing, furious, fury, indignant, passion, rage, vigorous.

204410 救 jiù: aid, assist, free somebody from danger, help, relieve, rescue, save.

204411 捻 (撚) niǎn, niē: assemble, delicate, dredge up, drive, fish out, hold, hold up, lead, made by twisting, matter, play tricks on or toy with, press, press with fingers, stop, stuff, take, tease, things twisted into a long slender form, toy with, trample, twirl in the fingers, twist with fingers, twisting.

204700 然 rán: afterwards, burn - fire, but, certainly, correct, fire, however, light, like that, like this, -ly, never, nevertheless, no mistake, pledge, promise, right, so, so called, such, suddenly, then, thus, yes, yet.

204700 然后 (然後) ránhòu: after that, afterwards, then.

204700 然而 rán'ér: however, but, however, yet.

205300 受 shòu: accept, bear, endure, get, passive marker, pleasant, receive, stand, stand to bear, subjected to, suffer.

206210 孩 hái: baby, child.

206210 家 (傢) jiā, jie, gū: -ary, businesses, capital, court, domestic, domicile, dwelling place, emperor, -er, every family, expert, family, group, home, house, household, husband or wife, -ian, individual, internal, -ist, married woman's maiden home, marry, measure word for stores and schools, minister and high official or theirs feud, my, nation, noun suffix for specialists - musician – revolutionary, patient, person, person engaged in a certain art or profession, person or family engaged in a certain trade, philosophical schools of pre-Han China, property, residence, school, settle down, sow grains, specialist in a certain field, stores, support a family, utensil.

207501 愛: Mentioned in some versions, but rep aced with the simplified 306300 爱.

207800 燃 rán: burn, combustion, ignite, light, light fire, raise hopes, spark off hopes, start debate

208310 窈 yǎo, yào: beauty, deep, elegant, obscure, quiet, refined, secluded, tranquil.

208600 溪 (谿) qī, xī: brook, creek, mountain stream, rivulet, stream.

209500 滋 zī: develop, excite, flourishing, grow, increase, moisten, multiply, nourish, this, thrive.

210000 上 shàng: above, appear, apply, attend - class or university, climb, fill, first - multiple parts, fix, go, go into, go to, go up, high position, higher, higher authorities, highest, in, install, last, lead, leader, make entrance, on, on top, place of honour, precedence, previous, previous or last week, promote, reach, send up, serve, superior, take part in activity, tighten, top, up, upon, upper, upper part, wind.

210000 上下 shàngxià: about, from top to bottom, high and low, length, old and new, old and young, or so, or thereabouts, relative superiority or inferiority, top and bottom, up and down.

210000 土 tǔ: clay, crude opium, dust, earth, indigenous, items made of earth, local, musical instrument, soil, unsophisticated.

210000 士 shì: bachelor, bodyguard, chess piece, commendable person, expert, first class military rank, gentleman, honorific, knight, non-commissioned officer, nurse, official, people between minister and common people, scholar, senior minister, sergeant, social stratum, soldier, specialist, warrior

210001 己 jǐ: 6th heavenly stem, closely related, hexa, one's own side, oneself, personal, private, self, sixth in order, themselves.

210001 已 yǐ: afterwards, already, finish, finished, later on, pass over, perish, stop, then, too much.

210010 卫 (衛) wèi: defend, guard, health, hygiene, protect, toilet.

210100 亡 wáng, wú: death, deceased, desert, destroy, die, flee, get lost, gone, lose, loss, missing, perish, run away, subjugate, unable to keep.

210100 亡为 wángwéi: miss action, Non-action.

210100 亡者 wángzhě: dead, deceased, missing soldiers in battle.

211000 仁 rén: benevolence, humane, kernel, kindness, sympathy.

nemonik-thinking.org

211000 仁义 (仁義) rényì: affable, benevolence, even-tempered, justice, kind-hearted, righteousness.

211000 开 (開) kāi: begin, blooming, boil, come undone, degrees Kelvin, driving, hold, initiate, open up, operate vehicle, pay, ratio, run, serve, start, turn on, write out a medical prescription.

211100 尺 chě, chǐ: acu-point, foot, measure one-third of a meter - foot, musical note on traditional Chinese scale, ruler, tape-measure, unit of length.

211100 平 píng: calm, draw - score, equal, even, flat, level, ordinary, peaceful, plain, suppress, tie - same score.

211100 户 (戶) hù: account, bank account, capacity for liquor, cave, census register, door, drinking capacity, family, family status, hinder, hole, home, house, household, personal or family occupation, social standing, stop.

211100 户牖 (戶牖) hùyǒu: door, door and window, home.

211100 未 wèi: 6th solar month, 8th earthly branch, 8th terrestrial branch, did not, have not, may not, not, not yet, year of the Sheep.

211100 未兆 wèizhào: unpredictable.

211100 未央 wèiyāng: close to the end, not ended, not yet over.

211100 未有 wèiyǒu: do not have, has never been, have not, is not, never occurring, never seen in past history, not, there is no, unprecedented, without.

211100 未知 wèizhī: unknown.

211100 未足 wèijù, wèizú: insufficient, less than, not foot, not much, not worth, unworthy.

211100 末 mò: blot out, commerce, curtain, dust, end, erase, final, final stage, humble, industry, inessential detail, insignificant, last, last – day, last stage, latter part, lower, minor detail, nonessential, opera role, powder, small, superficial, terminal, tip, tip of tree.

211100 本 běn: at first, basis, book, capital, current, edition, files, foundation, main, master copy, one's own, origin, originally, periodicals, present, root or source of things, root or stem of a plant, source, this.

211120 闭 (閉) bì: block up, close, end, obstruct, prohibit, shut, shut- door, stop, stop up.

211120 闭者 (閉 者) bìzhě: close by, shut, warden.

211201 志 (誌) zhì: ambition, annals, aspiration, aspire, bear in mind, desire, determination, goal, ideal, keep in mind, mark, measure, purpose, record, sign, the will, weigh, will, wish, write a footnote.

211202 忌 jì: abstain, avoid, dread, envious, envy, fear, give up, jealous, quit, scruple, taboo.

211202 忌讳 (忌諱) jìhuì: abstain from, avoid as taboo, avoid doing something, prohibit as taboo, taboo.

211301 忘 wáng, wàng: forget, miss, neglect, omit, overlook.

211310 过 (過) guō, guò: better than, celebrate - holiday, cross, defeat, done with, error, excessively, finished, get along, go across, go over, live one's life, mistake, over, pass by, pass through, pass time, passing, too, turn round.

211310 过于 (強大) guòyú: excessively, too, too much.

211310 过客 (過客) guòkè: passerby, passing traveller, sojourner, transient guest.

211310 过格(過格) guògé: exceed what is proper.

211310 闵 (閔) mǐn: anxious, compassion, condolences, confused, encourage, grieve, have mercy, incite, mixed, mourn, pity, sad, sorrowful, sympathize, urge on, worry.

211310 闵闵 (閔閔) mǐnmǐn: very confused, very lax, very worried.

212000 戶: Mentioned in some versions, but replaced with the simplified 211100 户.

212001 先 xiān: advance, ancestor, at first, before, deceased, earlier, elder generation, first, for the time being, former, in advance, late, lead, precede, predate, previous, prior, recede.

212001 先后 (先後) xiānhòu: early or late, in succession, one after another, priority, successively.

212001 老 lǎo: aged, all the time, always, become old, brother, dark colour, decrepit, deep colour, die, experienced, feeble, for a long time, former, great, hard meat, hardened, honour, long standing, long time, love, old, old people, original, outdated, overgrown, parents, past, prefix used before the surname or numeral indicating the order of birth - affection - familiarity, respect, retire from age, senile, short for Lao Zi, term of honour and respect for some feudal officials, thick, tough - meat, traditional, useless, venerable - person, very, veteran, weak, well-done, youngest.

nemonik-thinking.org

212001 老子 Lǎozi, Lǎozǐ: Chinese philosopher Lao Zi, daddy, father, founder of Taoism, I - used arrogantly or jocularly, I - your father - in anger or out of contempt, sacred book of Daoism.

212001 老子 Lǎozǐ: Lao Zi or Lao Tzu.

212001 老子之道德經 LǎozǐzhīDàodéjīng: Lao Zi's Dao De Jing or Lao Tzu's Tao Te Ching.

212010 功 gōng: accomplishment, achievement, good result, merit, meritorious deeds, physical work, result, service, skill, work – physics.

212010 功成 gōngchéng: achieve success and win recognition, not claim credit for oneself, off the ground, succeed.

212010 折 (摺) shé, zhē, zhé: accounts book, bend, break, change direction, convert - currency, convert into, convince, discount, fold - document, fracture, lose, loss, rebate, snap, tenth in price, theatrical scenes, tip out container, turn, turn back, turn upside-down, turnover, twist, winding.

212010 行 háng, hàng, héng, xíng, xìng: act, age - order of brothers, all right, apply, behaviour, capable, carry out, circulate, competent, conduct, current, do, effective, go, in circulation, journey, makeshift, move, OK, okay, perform, practice, profession, professional, relating to company, row, series, succeed, temporary, travel, visit, walk, will do.

212010 行者 xíngzhě: forerunner, itinerant monk, pedestrian, pioneer, travel, traveller, vanguard, walker.

212100 去 qù: after a verb of motion indicates movement away from the speaker, after certain verbs to indicate detachment or separation, apart, apart from in space or time, cast out, cause to go, depart to go, difference, get rid of, go, go away from, go to a place, leave, make somebody go, passed or elapsed time or an event, past, reject, remove, send, send somebody, went.

212100 并 (並), 併 bīng, bìng: also, altogether, amalgamate, and, annex, at the same time, besides, bring together, combine, completely, entirely, furthermore, get rid of, have, identical, join, merge, really, same, side by side, simultaneous, together, what's more.

212110 仿 (倣, 彷) fǎng: alike, as if, broad, copy, follow the example, hesitate, imitate, level, like, model for calligraphy, resemble, seemingly, similar, waver.

212110 判 pàn: clearly, conclude to judge, condemn, decide, different, discern, discriminate, distinguish, judge, obviously different, sentence.

212110 杤 lè, lì: achievements, being great, brambles, consider, corners, deeds, deliberate, edges, grain - wood, merits, think, thistles, thorn, corners, edges, wood texture.

212110 赤 chì: bare, communist, naked, red, scarlet, sincere.

212110 赤子 chìzǐ: newborn baby, ruler's subjects.

212200 位 wèi: binary bits such as 16-bit or 2 bytes, digit, location, persons, place, position, post, rank, seat, status, throne.

212200 坐 zuò: accused, airplane, bear fruit, because, face away, for the reason, go by, have the back towards, kick, kick back, place, place on fire, punished, put, recoil, ride, seat, seated, sink, sit, subside, take, take - bus, take a seat, travel, travel by, without cause.

212200 垃 lā: assist, break, bring up, canvass, carry, chat, convey by vehicles, destroy, drag, draw, empty bowels, garbage, haul, help, implicate, involve, lift, move - troops, owe, play instrument, press, pressgang, pull, refuse, rubbish, smash, solicit, transport, trash, tug, waste, win over.

212200 戎 róng: armaments, arms, army, army matters, forces, generic term for weapons, military affair, troops, weapon.

212200 戎马 (戎馬) róngmǎ: by extension, military horse, military matters, war horse.

212200 来 (來) lái, lài: about, appear, arise, around, arrive, cause to come, come from, come round, come up, coming, crop up, derive, ever since, future, next, return, take place.

212210 两 (兩) liǎng, liàng: both, several, some, two, couple, few, ounce, pair, some, tael, two, weight - 50 grams.

212210 两者 (兩者) liǎngzhě: both sides or parties.

212210 成 chéng: able, accomplish, achievement, act as, all right, as, be, be all right, because of, become, capable, competent, complete, conclude, considerable numbers or amounts, entire, established, finish, fixed, for, form, get married, help to achieve aim, help to bring about, hundreds and thousands, make, mature, mean, OK!, one tenth, pacification, pure, ready-made,

nemonik-thinking.org

renewed, result, ripen, serve as, set up, standing, successful, suppression, turn into, win.

212210 成功 chénggōng: succeed, success, successful.

212210 成名 chéngmíng: achieve personal fame and career, become famous, become well-known, come to fame make a name for oneself.

212210 执 (執) zhí: adhere, carry out, execute - plan, grasp, hold, hold in hand, hold on, keep, persist, stick to, take charge.

212300 达 (達) dá: achieve, amount, arrive, attain, clear, communicate, comprehensive, convey, current, dignity, distinguish, eminent, express, extend, general, go to, illustrious, influential, inform, intelligent, last, lead to, make, notify, pass through, reach, realize, recommend, slippery, smooth, thorough, thoroughly understand, understand.

213010 仍 réng: again, again and again, as ever, continuing, hence, keeping, occur frequently, remain, still, yet.

213010 伤 (傷) shāng: fed up, harm, hurt, impair, injure, injury, wound, fall ill.

213010 伤人 (傷人) shāngrén: hurt somebody's feelings, inflict injuries, injure health, injure somebody.

213100 攻 gōng: accuse, assault, attack, criticize, delve into, stud.

213110 均 jūn, yùn: all, average, balanced, equal, even, fair, uniform, without exception.

213200 弃 (棄) qì: abandon, discard, forsake, give up, reject, relinquish, throw away.

213300 俭 (儉) jiǎn: economical, frugal, needy, simple, temperate, thrifty.

213300 祅 yāo: calamity, calamity from terrestrial disorder, disasters, erroneous variant of xiān 祆, evil spirit, flourishing, goblin, luxuriant, prosperous, witchcraft.

213300 类 (類) lèi, lì: analogous, analogy, bias, category, class, example, fault, generally, group, in the main, kind, like, mostly, reason by, regulations, resemble, rules, sacrifice, sacrificial rites, similar, sort, to heaven, type.

213300 返 fǎn: restore, return, revert.

213301 洸 guāng, huáng: glitter, high wave, observe sea, sparkle, sparkling water.

nemonik-thinking.org

213302 恐 kǒng: afraid, anxiety, apprehensive, fear, frightened, guess, scared.

213310 将 (將) jiāng, jiàng, qiāng: checkmate, command, commander, commander-in-chief - military, desire, future, future tense - will - shall, general - military, get, going to, invite, just a short while ago, king - chess piece, lead, prepared, ready, request, shall, take, use, were, will, with.

213310 将军 (將軍) jiāngjūn: challenge, check or checkmate, commander, embarrass, general- military, high-ranking military officer, put somebody on the spot.

213310 邻国 (鄰國) línguó: bordering country, neighbouring countries, surrounding countries.

213310 邻邦 (鄰邦) línbāng: adjacent country, neighbouring, neighbouring state.

213310 郊 jiāo: open spaces, outskirts, suburban area, waste land.

213400 济 (濟) jǐ, jì: aid, cross - river, emergency assistance, ferry, free from danger, frugal, good for something, help, relieve, rescue, save.

213410 迹 (跡, 蹟) jì: footprint, impressions, indication, mark, remains, sign, trace, track, vestige.

213510 热 (熱) rè: ardent, craze, eager, envious, fad, fervent, fever, heat up, hot - weather, restless, temperature, thermal, warm up, warm-hearted, zeal.

214000 形 xíng: appear, appearance, body, entity, form, look, shape.

214001 饥 (飢, 饑) jī: famine, hunger, starving.

214021 驰 (馳) chí: disseminate, gallop, hurry, long for, quickly, run fast, speed, spread, swiftly, turn towards.

214021 驰骋 (馳騁) chíchěng: dash about in battlefield, gallop, rush headlong.

214100 牧 mù: breed livestock, govern, government official, herd, shepherd, tend cattle.

214100 牧养 (牧養) mùyǎng: raise animals, rear.

214202 虑 (慮) lù: anxiety, concerned, consider, think, think over, worry about.

214210 徐 xú: calm, composed, dignified, gentle, quietly, slow.

214210 炳 bǐng: bright, brilliant, depressed, glorious, luminous, remarkable, splendid, troubled, worried.

214310 阂 (閡) gāi, hé: alienation, blocked, cut off from, estrange, hamper, hinder, lack of understanding, not in communication, obstruct, prevent, separated.

214401 流 liú: banish, circulate, class, degenerate, disseminate, drift, exile, flow, grade, move, rate, spread, stream of water.

215001 纪 (紀) jǐ, jì: age, annals, chronological record of events, discipline, end, era, essentials, family name, from memory, guiding principle, handle, historical account, key link, law, limit, manage, Middle Ages, note, order, period, period of twelve years, record, servant, threads, threads of silk.

215010 物 wù: content, creature, environment, essence, matter, object, other people, outside world, produce, property, substance, thing.

215010 物质 wùzhì: matter.

215210 称 (稱) chèn, chēng, chèng: address, address, appellation, balanced, brand, call, commend, consider, estimate, fit, match, name, praise, raise, say, start, state, steelyard, suit, suitable, symmetrical, weigh, well-off.

215301 袭 (襲) xí: according, air raid, as before, as usual, attack, carry on, convention, funeral robes, in the light of, inherit, model, pattern, raid, still, suit of clothes, suits, surprise attack.

216100 饮 (飲) yǐn, yìn: drink, kind of drink, swallow.

216100 饮食 (飲食) yǐnshí: food and drink.

216410 遂 suí, suì: achieve, as one wishes, complete, comply with, consequently, finally, follow along, forthwith, fulfil, hence, proceed, reach, satisfy, succeed, then, thereupon, unexpectedly.

220000 口 kǒu: age of draft animal, bites, cannons, cut, department, domestic animals, edge of knife, entrance, gate, gateway, hole, mouth, mouthfuls, open end, opening, people, rim, section, wells.

220000 止 zhǐ: block, desist, detain, halt, hinder, merely, obstruct, only, prohibit, put a stop to, rest, stop, till, to, until, up to.

220001 屯 tún, zhūn: accumulate, assemble, block, camp, collect, difficult, garrison, grudge, hamlet, hard, have garrison troops open up wasteland and grow food grain, hill, hoard, pier, quarter - troops, slow, station, station - troops, station soldiers, stingy, stock, store, store up, surplus, troop station, village.

220001 屯屯 túntún, zhūnzhūn: camp, extreme surplus, hamlet, station, stores, village.

nemonik-thinking.org

220110 市 shì: buy, city, deal in, exchange, fair, market, municipality, sell, town, trade, weights and measures.

220410 雨 yǔ, yù: rain, rainy.

221001 兄 xiōng: brother, courteous form of address, elder brother.

221001 四 sì: 4, four, IV.

221001 四大 sìdà: airing views fully, four elements - earth - water - fire - air, four freedoms - speaking out freely - airing views fully - holding great debates - writing big-character posters, holding great debates and writing big character posters, speaking out freely.

221001 四达 (四達) sìdá: environment, four reach, surroundings.

221001 四邻 (四鄰) sìlín: one's nearest neighbours, surrounding neighbours.

221010 刑 xíng: appearance, body, corporal punishment, cut, dig, form, go on a punitive expedition, instrument of torture, kill, law, penalty, punish, punishment, sample, sentence, shape - by punishment as in behaviourism, term of astrology, torture.

221100 亚 (亞) yā, yà: Asia, bend, close, hang down, inferior, lower than, near, next to, press, press down, second, sub-, sub-tropical, ugly.

221100 企 qǐ: enterprise or company, look forward, plan, stand on tiptoe.

221100 共 gōng, gòng: all, altogether, common, general, in all, in a while, joint, merge, mutual, respect, share, span with the hand, supply, surround, together, total.

221100 共之璧 gòngzhībì: disc of jade with hole at centre - symbol.

221100 壮 (壯) zhuàng: admire, big, bolster, brave, firm, grand, grandeur, grown-up, healthy, heroic, injure, large, robust, stout, strengthen, strong, sturdy, tall and big.

221100 央 yāng: beg, centre, conclude, disaster, end, entreat, far, finish, plead, run out, stop.

221100 尘 (塵) chén: ashes, cinders, dirty thing, dust, earth, human world, stain, trace, world.

221100 计 (計) jì: calculate, compute, count, gauge, measured, plan, plot, reckon, ruse, scheme, stratagem, strategy.

221120 刺 cì, qì: assassinate, irritate, murder, pierce, prick, prod, stab, sting, thorn, thrust, whoosh.

221200 式 shì: ceremony, example, fashion, form, formula, pattern, posture, principle, ritual, rule, style, system, type.

221210 闲 (閑) xián: chatty, digressive, idle, leisure, lying idle, not busy, not in use, quiet, spare time, unoccupied, unused, defend, enclosure, fence, guard, idle, leisure, not busy, unoccupied.

221210 闲聊 xiánliáo: chat, idle gossip.

222010 印 yìn: chop, conform, engrave, image, mark, print, seal, stamp, stamp - post, tally, trace.

222100 兵 bīng: arms, army, fighting, force, military, soldiers, troops, war, warlike, warrior, weapons.

222100 兵革 bīnggé: military equipment, military weapons.

222100 台 (檯, 臺, 颱) tāi, tái, yí: broadcasting station, desk, pedestal, platform, respectful address, stage, stand, station, support, table, term of address - you in letters, terrace, tower, typhoon, unit, vehicles – machines.

nemonik-thinking.org

222100 坏 (壞) huài, péi, pī: awful, bad, break down, broken, dirty trick, evil, evil idea, extreme, go off, rotten, ruin, spoiled.

222101 兑 (兌) duì, ruì, yuè: add - liquid, add - water, blend, cash, convert, exchange, one of the E ght Trigrams, symbolizing swamp.

222101 观 (觀) guān, guàn: advise, appearance, behold, cognition, concept, examine, knowledge, look at, observe, palace gate, platform, point of view, prospect, see, Taoist monastery, view, watch, watchtower.

222110 希 xī: cherish, curious, expect, few, hope, infrequent, rare, scarce, seldom, strive for, uncommon.

222110 芬 fēn, fén: aroma, fragrance, perfume, sweet smell.

222110 财 (財) cái: financial resources, money, property, resources, riches, valuables, wealth.

222200 快 kuài: almost, clever, fast, forthright, frank, gratified, happy, make haste, plain-spoken, pleasant, pleased, quick, rapid, rate, sharp of knives or wits, soon, speed, straightforward, swift.

222200 谷 (穀) gòu, gǔ, hún, lù, nòu, yù: cereal, confluence, corn, difficult, dilemma, good, gorge, grain, kind, live, lucky, millet, mountain stream, obituary notice, paper mulberry, pool, poor, provide for, ravine, salary, stream, trough, unhusked rice, unite, valley.

222200 谷神 gǔshén: Ceres, corn god, harvest God.

222200 谷神不死 gǔshēnbùsǐ: eternal downward force, gravity, immortal valley spirit.

222200 还 (還) hái, huán, xuán: also, as early as, besides, counter offer, else, even more, fairly, in addition, more, not yet, passably - good, pay back, rebound, repay, return, still in progress, still more, strike back, yet.

222210 讷 (訥) nà, nè: large, mumble, slow speech, speak cautiously, stammer.

222301 恶 (惡) è, wū, wù: ashamed, bad, barren land, coarse, culprit, detest, dirty, discomfiting, disgust, dislike, envious, evil, exclamation, fault, fear, ferocious, fierce, foul, harm, hate, how, loathe, nausea, slander, taboo, ugly, venomous, very, vice, vicious, villain, vulgar, what, where, wicked, wickedness.

223010 苉 hū, wū, wù: annual herb, dim, fluorine, organic compound, suddenly, trance, vegetable.

223020 抑 yì: control, curb, hinder, keep down, lowered, or, press down, repress, restrain, restrict.

223100 负 (負) fù: arrears, bear, carry on back or shoulder, defeated, enjoy, have, lose, negative, owe, rely on, shoulder, suffer, turn one's back, bear, burden, carry, carry on one's back, load, lose, negative – math.

223200 丧 (喪) sāng, sàng: corpse, defeated, die, flee, funeral, lose, lose - by death, mourn, mourning.

223200 丧事 (喪事) sāngshì: funeral arrangements.

223200 丧礼 (喪禮) sānglǐ: dutiful, funeral, funeral rite, obedient, obsequies, servile.

223200 败 (敗) bài: decline, defeat, fail, lose, loss, wither.

223200 近 jì, jìn: approach, approximately, close, intimate, near.

223210 贫 (貧) pín: deficient, garrulous, inadequate, lack, poor, poverty-stricken, short of, verbose.

223301 怠 dài: careless, disrespect, idle, lazy, neglect, negligent, remiss.

223400 迷 mì, mí, mèi: absorbed, bewilder, bewitch, charm, confused, crazy about, enthusiast, fan, fascinated, infatuate, lost.

224101 乘 chéng, shèng: ascend, avail, Buddhist sect or creed, chariot, chase, four, four horse military chariot, generic term for history books, historical works, make use, mount, multiply - mathematics, numeracy adjunct for vehicles, pursue, ride, ride, take - e.g. bus, take advantage, travel, use.

224101 乘乘 chéngchéng: much travel.

224201 疵 cī, jì, zhài, zī: blemish, defect, disease, fault, flaw.

224310 敝 bì: broken, defeated, destroy, exhaust, my, poor, ragged, rubbish, ruined, shabby, tattered, waste, worn out.

224400 渊 (淵) yuān: abyss, broad, bubble up, deep, deep lake, deep water, erudite, gush forth, profound, surge up.

225100 彼 bǐ: another one, other side, that, there, those.

225100 须 (須, 鬚) xū: await, beard, feeler, feeler of an insect, have to, moustache, must, necessary, tassel, wait.

225300 颂 (頌) róng, sòng: acclaim, eulogy, extol, hymn, laud, ode, praise, praise in writing, song, wish in letter.

229300 缪 (繆) jiū, liǎo, miào, miù, móu, mù: bind, cheat, community, curl up, defraud, distinct, false, join in a common effort, prepare, pretend, reverent, silent, solemn, twist, unite efforts, wind around, wring, wrong.

nemonik-thinking.org

229600 繆: Mentioned in some versions, but replaced with the simplified 229300 缪.

230000 中 zhōng, zhòng: affected, agreeable, all right, amidst, among, attain, central, centre, China, Chinese, during, fall, fit, good for, halfway, hit, hit by, hit target, impartial, in, in the midst of, in the process of, inside, intermediate, intermediator, mean, mediocre, medium, mid, middle, moderate, OK, suffer, suitable, sustain, well, while doing something, within.

230000 中有 zhōngyǒu: in, know what's what.

231010 师 (師) shī: army, division - military, example, expert, master, model, pattern, skilled person, specialist, teacher, tutor.

231010 而 ér, néng: ability, addition, and, and then, and yet, as well as, but, but also, but not, can, change into, co-ordination, further, furthermore, his, how could, how is it possible, however, if, in case, into the bargain, like, moreover, of, seem, shows causal relation, shows change of state, shows contrast, the, to, while, yet, yet not, you, your.

231010 而为 (而為, 而爲) érwéi: and the, do the best one could.

nemonik-thinking.org

231010 而后 (而後) érhòu: after that, then.

231010 而已 éryǐ: just, nothing more, only, that is all.

231011 吔 yē, yě: amazement, exclamations – ah - oh, phonetic - yeah, sigh, surprise.

231100 吏 lì: Confucian gentleman, government official, magistrate.

231100 虫 (蟲) chóng, huǐ: generic term for animals, insect, invertebrate, worm.

231100 贞 (貞) zhēn: chaste, chastity, faithful, loyal, pure, virginity, virtuous.

231110 芮 ruì, ruò: cotton wadding, edge of water, small, soft, supple, thongs of a shield, tiny, water's edge.

231201 忠 zhōng: devoted, devotion, faithful, fidelity, honest, loyalty.

231201 忠信 érhòu: faithful, faithful and honest, have known each other long, loyal and sincere.

232101 恍 huǎng: blurred, dejected, despondent, disappointed, distracted, flurried, frightened, frustrated, indistinct, mad, no peace of mind, panic-stricken, restless, sudden, wild'

232201 视 (視) shì: inspect, look, observe, regard, see, treat, watch.

233100 伿 chì, yǐ: dangerous, dull-witted, foolish, idiotic, motionless, silly, stagnant, standstill, static, still, stupid.

233100 俨 (儼) yǎn: dignified, grave, just like, majestic, not frivolous, orderly, respectful, solemn.

233100 质 (質) zhí, zhì: character, hostage, material, matter, nature, pawn, plain, pledge, quality, question, substance.

233110 独 (獨) dú: alone, independent, only, single, solely, solitary.

233110 独立 (獨立) dúlì: independent, on one's own, stand alone.

233200 俗 sú: coarse, colloquially, common, convention, custom, habit, ordinary, popular, secular, social custom, unrefined, vulgar.

233200 俗人 súrén: common people, laity - i.e. not priests, ordinary person, vulgar person.

233201 悦 (悅) yuè: contented, delighted, gratified, happy, pleased.

233210 迎 yíng, yìng: face, facing, forge ahead - in the face of difficulties, greet, meet, receive, welcome.

nemonik-thinking.org

233300 柢 dǐ: base, bottom of object, broad outline, foundation, fountainhead, general idea, origin, root, source.

234300 祇 qí, zhǐ: but, earth-spirit, god of the earth, merely, only, peace.

242101 览 (覽) lǎn: inspect, look at, look over, perceive, read, see, view.

242110 刿 (劌) guì: cut, injure, meet, stab, stick on.

242200 贤 (賢) xián: able, clever, good, honorific used for a person of the same or a younger generation, knowledgeable, moral conduct, worthy or virtuous person.

243100 顺 (順) shùn: agreeable, align, along, arrange, as one wishes, careful, cautious, coherent, conveniently, embellish, favourable, follow, go along, go well, if convenient, in passing, in same direction, instruct, make reasonable, mild, obey, on the way, order, polish, proper order, prudent, put in order, readable, reason, reasonable, same direction, submit, successful, successively, teach, with, yield to.

250000 出 chū: appear, break forth, come out, depart, dramas, emerge, exceed, give out, go beyond, go out, happen, issue, leave, occur, operas, out, pay out, plays, produce, put forth, rise, send out, stand.

250000 出于 (出於) chūyú: due to, out of, proceed from, start from, stem from.

250000 出口 chūkǒu: exit, export, leave port - ship, speak, utter.

250000 出生 chūshēng: born.

250000 出生入死 chūshēngrùsǐ: brave, from the cradle to the grave, risk one's life, through fire and water, willing to risk life and limb.

250000 出言 chūyán: remark, speak, speech, spoken words, words.

255000 绌 (絀) chù, zhuó: crimson silk, deficiency, inadequate, insufficient, not enough, sew, stitch.

300000

300000 三 sān, sàn: 3, few, several, third, three.

300000 三十 sānshí: 30, thirty

300000 三宝 sānbǎo: three treasures. Lao Zi's three treasures include compassion, frugality, and humbleness [67]. In Buddhism, the triratna. The triad of Buddha, Dharma, and Sangha.

301010 与 (與) yú, yǔ, yù: against, and, associate, careful, final interrogative particle expression doubt or surprise, for, get along, give, grant, have a hand in, have dealings, help, make contact, offer, on good terms, participate, send, support, take part, to, together, wait, with.

301210 母 mú, mǔ, wú, wǔ: concave, female, female elders, female relatives, mother, origin, parent, source, mother.

302010 毋 móu, wú: don't, no, not, not as good as, unnecessary, without.

302010 马 (馬) mǎ: horse, horse - chess piece.

302010 马王堆 (馬王堆) Mǎwángduī: Mawangdui in Changsha Hunan, Mawangdui version of Lao Zi's Dao De Jing.

302100 专 (專) zhuān: concentrated, dominate, expert, focused on one thing, for a particular person, monopoly, occasion, particular to something, purpose, specialized, take sole possession.

302111 抗 kàng: anti-, combat, contend, defy, fight, match for, oppose, refuse, reject, resist.

nemonik-thinking.org

302210 奈 nài: bear, but, deal with, despite, endure, how, how can one help, however, regret, stand, tackle, this, what.

302210 奈何 nàihé: cope, deal with, do something to somebody, how, how to deal with, no avail, what about, what is to be done.

302310 亲 (親) qīn, qìng, xīn: bride, close, closely related, dear, first-hand, in favour of, in person, intimate, kiss, loving, marriage, next-of-kin, one's flesh and blood, parent, parents-in-law of one's offspring, personally, pro-, related by blood, relation, relative.

302400 泣 lì, qì, sè: cry, sob, weep.

303020 扔 rēng, rèng: abandon, cast, cast aside, destroy, force, hurl, pull, suddenly, throw, throw away, toss, wreck.

303110 动 (動) dòng: act, change, happen, move, stir, travelling, use.

303110 动动 dòngdòng: move extremely.

303110 好 hǎo, hào: apt, easy, excellent, fine, fond, good, liable, like, likely, proper, so, suffix indicating completion or readiness, very, well.

303110 字 zì: character, courtesy name for males aged 20, letter, pronunciation, symbol, word, wording, written pledge.

303111 投 tóu: cast, fling, invest, jump, pitch, post, put in, ram in, seek, send, throw, throw oneself.

303210 宗 zōng: aim, ancestor, ancestry, batches, cases - medical or legal, clan, faction, family, forbears, forefathers, great master, group, intention, items, lineage, model, model - academic or artistic, object, purpose, reservoirs, school, sect, temple.

303210 拔 bá: destroy, draw, draw out by suction, pick, promote, pull away, pull out, pull up, seize, select, stand out above level, surpass, uproot.

303210 拔拔 bábá: pulled away extremely

303210 疠 (癘) lì: butcher, encourage, go through the mill, kill, leprosy, pestilence, plague, slaughter, sore, steel oneself, temper oneself, ulcer, urge.

303301 没 (沒) me, méi, mò: confiscate, die, disappear, do not, drowned, end, expropriate, has not, have not, hide, inferior, inundate, last, less than, negative prefix for verbs, never, no, none, not, not as good as, not have, overflow, rise beyond, sink, submerge, there is not, vanish, without.

303310 泰 tài: big, exalted, grand, great, most, peaceful, safe, superior.

304210 学 (學) xué: imitate, knowledge, learning, mimic, -ology, school, science, study.

304210 学者 (學者) xuézhě: educated person, knowledgeable, scholar.

304300 废 (廢) fèi: abandon, abolish, abrogate, crippled, depose, disable, discard, disuse, give up, invalid, maim, oust, reject, terminate, useless, waste, waste.

304300 笑 xiào: giggle, laugh, smile, snicker.

304410 涤 (滌) dí: clean, cleanse, clear away, cowshed, purify, sweep, wash, wipe.

304410 涤除 (滌除) díchú: do away with, eliminate, wash away.

305110 欤 (歟) yú: final particle expressing - question - doubt - surprise - admiration, how could one fail to exercise caution, secular.

305200 叛 pàn: betray, bright, promising, rebel, rebellion, rebellious, revolt.

mnemonic-thinking.org

305310 矜 jīn, guān, qín: arrogant, boast, brag, conceited, egoistic, esteem, feel sorry, have mercy, pity, prim, reserved, restrained, self-important, self-praise, self-respect, show sympathy, sympathize.

305710 撚: Mentioned in some versions, but replaced with the simplified 204411 捻.

306300 爱 (愛) ài: affection, apt, care, cherish, daughter, enjoy, favour, fond, friendly affect, greedy, grudge, habit, highly possible, kind heartedness, liable, like, love, stint, take pity, treasure.

310000 丰 (豐) fēng: abundant, appearance and carriage of a person, bountiful, bumper harvest, buxom, full, good-looking, great, lush, plenty, rich.

310000 王 wáng, wàng, yù: best or strongest of its kind, chief, grand, great, head, king, monarch, reign, royal, rule, ruler.

310000 王侯 wánghóu: aristocracy, marquises, nobility, princes.

310000 王公 wánggōng: aristocracy, dukes, princes.

310000 王弼 Wángbì: Chinese philosopher Wang Bi (226–249 AD), version of Lao Zi's Dao De Jing.

nemonik-thinking.org

310100 主 zhǔ: advocate, betoken, chief owner, God, have a definite view, host, idea, in favour, indicate, individual or party concerned, leader, lord, main, manage, master, opinion, own, owner, person concerned, possessor, presage, primary, principal, signify, stand for, subjective, take charge, take charge, trump card in card games, view.

310100 玉 yù: gem, jade, precious stone.

310110 寺 sì: Buddhist temple, court, government bureau, monastery, mosque, office, temple.

311000 五 wǔ: 5, five.

311000 五味 wǔwèi: all kinds of flavours, five flavours - sweet - sour - bitter - pungent - salty, five tastes, flavours.

311000 五色 wǔsè: five colours - blue - yellow - red - white – black, garish, multi-coloured, rainbow.

311000 五音 wǔyīn: five initial consonants of Chinese phonetics, five notes of Chinese music, five notes of pentatonic scale - do - re - mi - sol – la.

311000 左 zuǒ: bigoted, contrary, different, differing, east, heretical, improper, incorrect, left, left - politics, left side, opposite, progressive, queer, radical, revolutionary, unorthodox, wrong.

311000 左右 zuǒyòu: approximately, attendant, control, influence, left and right.

311000 生 shēng: alive, bear, birth, born, crude, extremely, foster, generate, get, give birth, give rise to, grow, life, lifetime, light a fire, live, living, originate, pupil, raw, stiff, student, uncooked, unfamiliar, unripe, very.

311000 生日 shēngrì: birthday.

311000 生生 shēngshēng: breed unceasingly, by force, compulsorily, generation after generation, live extremely, multiply, suffix.

311000 车 chē, jū: car, carriage, carry in cart, cart, castle, chariot, lathe, lift water by waterwheel, machine, piece of chess, pump water, rook in chess, shape, shape with a lathe, turn, vehicle, war chariot, wheeled machine.

311010 弓 gōng: arched, bend, bow - weapon, curved.

311010 用 yòng: apply, drink, eat, employ, expense or outlay, function, have to, hence, need, operate, require, therefore, use, useful, usefulness, utilise.

311010 用人 yòngrén: employ others, in need of staff, leader, make the best use of staff, manage people, servant, understaffed.

311010 用兵 yòngbīng: command troops, direct, direct military operations, movement of military forces, plan, resort to arms, use military forces.

311100 全 quán: all, complete, entire, every, full, intact, keep whole or intact, maintain, perfect, preserve, total, whole.

311100 圣 (聖) kū, shèng: adoration, extreme high, holy, lofty, sacred, sage, saint, sublime, title for Emperor, worship.

311100 圣人 (聖人) shèngrén: reigning Emperor, sage, saint, wise person.

311100 气 (氣) qì: air, anger, breath, bullying, enraged, flavour, fly into a rage, fresh air, gas, get angry, insult, make somebody angry, maltreatment, mood, odour, smell, steam, vapour, vital breath, vital or bodily energy, weather.

311120 鸟 (鳥) diǎo, niǎo: bird.

311200 江 jiāng: large river, river, river - not the name of a specific river.

312010 存 cún: balance - account, be, be leftover, check, cherish, deposit, exist, harbour, keep, live, place for safe keeping, preserve, remain, retain, safe place, save, store, survive.

312010 巧 qiǎo: as it happens, clever, coincidentally, ingenious, intelligent, off hand, opportunely, skilful, skill, speech, timely.

312010 狂 jué, kuáng: arrogant, conceited, crazy, insane, mad, violent, wild.

312100 至 zhì: arrive, best, come, extreme, first-rate, go, most, optimal, perfect, reach, till, to, until, utmost, very.

312100 至 坚 (至 堅) zhìjiān: firm, hard, hardest.

312100 至 于 (至 於) zhìyú: as, as for, as to, for, go so far as to, the.

312100 至 柔 zhìróu: soft, softest.

312110 技 jì: ability, ingenuity, skill, talent, technique.

312110 技巧 jìqiǎo: skill, technique.

312120 报 (報) bào: announce, declare, inform, newspaper, recompense, repay, report, requite, respond, retaliate, revenge, tell.

312120 报怨 (報怨) bàoyuàn: avenge a grievance, complain, pay back a score, requite, revenge.

312200 妄 wàng: abnormal, absurd, arrogant, extraordinary, false, fantastic, foolish, ludicrous, presumptuous, rash, reckless, ridiculous, unusual.

312200 金 jīn, jìn: generic term for lustrous and ductile metals, gold, highly respected, metals in general, money, musical instrument, precious, respected.

312200 金玉 jīnyù: gold and jade, precious, precious stones and metals, treasures.

312201 远 (遠) yuǎn, yuàn: difference, distance, distance oneself from, distant, far, far away, forever, keep away, long time, much, not close, profound, remote.

312300 举 (舉) jǔ: act, choose, cite, elect, enumerate, hold up, lift, name, raise.

312300 泮 pàn: bank, disperse, fall apart, melt, side.

313020 邪 shé, xié, xú, yá, yé, yú: abnormal, demonic, depraved, evil, heretical, heterodox, iniquitous, irregular, misfortune, nefarious, perverse, unfortunately, unhealthy, unhealthy influences that cause disease, vicious, wrong.

nemonik-thinking.org

313100 灵 (靈) líng, lìng: agile, alert, bier, bright, clever, coffin, deity, departed soul, easy, effective, efficacious, elf, fairy, hearse, intelligence, nimble, of the deceased, quick, sensitive, soul, spirit, spiritual world, sprite.

313100 牢 láo, lào, lóu: fast, firm, hold for animals, jail, pen, prison, sacrifice, sacrificial feast, secure, stable, sturdy.

313100 表 biǎo: administer medicine, appear, chart, cousin, display, example, express, exterior, external, family relationship via females, form, gauge, graph, list or table, manifest, memorial, meter - measuring, model, outside, show, surface, table, watch, wrist or pocket watch, wristwatch.

313110 季 jì: fourth or youngest amongst brothers, last month of a season, period, quarter of year, season, seasonal crop yields, youngest.

313110 季子 jìzǐ: period of two or three months, youngest brother.

313120 陈 (陳) chén, zhèn: arrange, display, exhibit, explain, lay out, mass, narrate, old, plead, stale, state, station, tell.

nemonik-thinking.org

313121 施 shī, shǐ, yí, yì: act, apply, bestow, bring, carry out, display, distribute, do, enforce, execute, exert, give, grant, name, use.

313200 养 (養) yǎng, yàng: breed, bring up - children, convalesce, cultivate, form, foster, give birth, keep in good repair, keep pets, maintain, raise - animals, rear, recuperate, support.

313200 定 dìng: calm, certainly, decide, definitively, determine, established, fixed, order - merchandize, set, settle, stable, surely.

313200 迭 dié: again and again, alternate, frequently, repeatedly.

313201 设 (設) shè: arrange, build, display, envisage, establish, found, plan, set up, suppose.

313210 挫 cuò: bend back, broken bone, chop down, damage, dampen, defeat, fail, file, frustrate, grind, lower, lower the tone, obstructed, oppress, push down, repress, subdue.

313220 势 (勢) shì: appearance, authority, circumstances, conditions, feature, force, form, gesture, influence, male genitals, momentum, opportunity, posture,

nemonik-thinking.org

potential, power, sign, situation, state of affairs, tendency, trend.

313220 除 chú, shū, zhù: apart from, besides, clean, confer an official, divide, do away with, eliminate, except, exclude, exterminate, get rid of, in addition, mend, not including, remove, repair, step, steps leading to a house, steps of palace, sweep, wipe, wipe out, with the exception.

313300 巠 jīng, xíng: flowing water, fluid, liquid, streams running underground.

313300 法 fǎ: Buddhism, Buddhist teaching, follow, law, legalist, magic, method, model, regulation, rule, statute, style, technique, way.

313300 法令 fǎlìng: decree, ordinance.

313300 法物 fǎwù: instrument used by the guard of honour of an emperor, musical instrument used in ancestral temples.

313310 病 bìng: ailment defect, disease, fall ill, fault, heart, hurt, illness, problem, sickness, taken ill, weakness.

313310 病 bìng: weak.

313310 病病 bìngbìng: very weak.

313400 送 sòng: accompany, carry, deliver, dispatch, escort, gift, give, present with, see off, send off, take.

314002 虎 hǔ, hù: brave, fierce, tiger, vigorous.

314112 能 nái, nài, néng, tái, tài, xióng: ability, able, can, can possibly, capable, competent, energy, may, permitted, power, skill.

314112 能无 néngwú: cannot.

314112 能无离 néngwúlí: cannot, inseparable, separate.

314112 能毋离 néngwúlí: cannot, inseparable, separate.

314200 极 (極) jí: again, anxiously, exceedingly, exhaust, extreme, farthest point, fast, final, furthest, highest - position - norm – standard, outmost, pole - geography - physics, principle, punish, reach, repeatedly, respectfully, ridgepole, study deeply, throne, top, utmost, very.

314200 耘 yún: weed.

314200 耘耘 yúnyún: confused, disorderly, diverse, numerous.

314210 柔 róu: flexible, gentle, pliant, soft, supp e, yielding.

314210 柔弱 róuruò: delicate, weak.

314300 威 wēi: august, authority, dignified, dominate, force, menace, might, pomp, power, powerful, prestige, threat.

314300 较 (較) jiào, jué: clearly - different, comparatively, compare, contrast, dispute, distinct, fairly, haggle over, markedly, more, preposition comparing difference in degree, quibble, rather.

314410 梁 (樑) liáng: beam of roof, bridge, rafters, ridge, surname.

315200 致 (緻) zhì, zhuì: achieve, appeal, cause, close, concentrate, convey, delicate, deliver, density, devote, enrol, extend, extensive, fine, give, give rise, incur, interest, invite, lay down, meticulous, pay, present, result, return, send, so that, take in, work for.

315200 致坚 zhìjiān: concentrate, hard, hardest.

315200 致柔 zhìróu: concentrate, soft, softest.

315210 素 sù: always, constituent, element, essence, ever, formerly, modest, nature, normally, plain, raw silk, unadorned, usually, vegetable, vegetarian, vegetarian food, vitamin, white, white silk.

315210 袤 xié: evil, monstrous, slit in garment to aid movement, strange.

315300 案 àn: bench, case - law, desk, file, incident, legal case, plan, propose, record, scheme, table.

315400 深 shēn: close, dark colour, deep, depth, difficult, extreme, far, far of in time, greatly, intimate, late, long after something began, penetrating, profound, thorough-going, very.

316110 骄 (驕) jiāo, xiāo: arrogant, conceited, haughty, insufferably, pride, proud, spirited horse.

316400 数 (數) cù, shǔ, shù, shuò: calculate, count, criticize, destiny, detail, enumerate, exceptional, fate, few, figure, frequently, list, number, rank, repeatedly, several.

316400 数者 (數者) shǔzhě: accountant, count.

31860 經 jīng: classic.

320000 日 mì, rì: daily, date, day, day by day, day of the month, day time, every day, sun, time, with each passing day.

320000 日常 rìcháng: daily, everyday — common.

320000 日益 rìyì: day by day, increasingly, more and more, more and more with each passing day.

320000 日 yuē: call, means, name, named, say, speak, states.

nemonik-thinking.org

320000 正 zhēng, zhèng: adjust, centre, chief, correct, due, exactly, first month of the lunar year, greater than zero, honest, just, just in time, just right, just suit the purpose, main, major, middle, normal, observe, ongoing, perfect, plus, positive, precise, principal, principle, proper, pure, pure colour, rectify, regular, regulate, right, right now, right side, rule, sharp, standardized, standards, straight, true, unmixed, upright.

320000 正统 zhèngtǒng: orthodox.

320000 甘 gān: fortunate, pleasant, sweet, tasty, willingly.

320000 甘露 gānlù: manna, sweet, sweet dew.

320000 露 lòu, lù: betray, dew, expose, juice, nectar, outdoors - not under cover, reveal, show, syrup.

320010 可 kě, kè: able, -able, approve, but, can, certainly, fit, may, neither very good or bad, particle used for emphasis - very, permissible, permit, possibly can, suit, worthy, yet.

320010 可以 kěyǐ: able, can, may, permissible, possible, would be willing.

321000 右 yòu: orthodox, right, right - politics, right – side, right-hand, right-wing, west.

321000 在 zài: action in progress, alive, at, be, before verbs - immediately involved in, belong, consist in, depend, during, exist, in, in course of, in the middle of doing, join, lie in, live, living, located at, member, on, process, remain, rest, stay.

321000 年 nián: age, annual, era, harvest, new year, person's age, year.

321000 归 (歸) guī, kuì: back, come together, converge, get married - woman, give back, go back, join, put under somebody's care, re-join one's unit, resign, return, return to original profession, revert to, set back, surrender.

321000 归于 guīyú: affiliated, attribute, belong, incline towards, result in something, tend to.

321000 归根 (歸根) guīgēn: go back to one's roots, in a nutshell, in a word, return home, return home after a lifetime's absence, return to one's native place after a long stay in an alien land, sum up.

321000 白 bái, bó: angry stare, anti-communist, blank, bright, clear, empty, explain, free of charge, funeral, gratuitous, in vain, make clear, mispronounced, no avail, plain, pure, reactionary, snowy, spoken lines in opera, stare coldly, state, turn white, unblemished, vernacular, waste effort, white, without result, write wrong character, wrongly spelled.

321000 石 dàn, shí: measure for grain, mineral, musical instrument, one hundred litres, rock, stone, stone inscription, ten pecks.

321000 耳 ěr, réng: and that is all, both sides, ear, ear of utensil, ear-like thing, handle - archaeology, just, merely, only, side.

321000 耳目 ěrmù: eyes and ears, information, knowledge, somebody's attention or notice, spy.

321000 耳聋 (耳聾) ěrlóng: deaf, deafness.

321001 异 (異) yì: different, discriminate, distinguish, exotic, extraordinary, hetero-, other, raise, separate, stop, strange, surprising, unusual.

321001 芜 (蕪) wú: grassland, luxurious growth of weeds, miscellaneous, overgrown with weeds, weed.

321010 加 jiā: add, append, augment, empower, increase, not consider, one after another, plus, put in, reinforce, strengthen.

nemonik-thinking.org

321010 句 jù, gōu: clause, mention, phrases or lines of verse, say a few words, sentence, syntax, tender bud, two lines of verse.

321010 召 shào, zhào: assemble, beckon, call, call together, convene, convent, imperial decree, monastery, send for, summon, temple.

321010 扣 (釦) kòu: arrest, buckle, button, confiscate, cover - with a bowl etc., deduct - money, detain, discount, fasten, frame, knock, knot, put aside, put down, rap, smash or spike a ball, strike, tag a label on somebody - figuratively, tap.

321100 合 hé, gě: 1st note of pentatonic scale, add up, close, coincide, combine, conform, conjunction - astronomy, equal, equivalent, fit, gather, in keeping with, join, measure for dry grain equal to one-tenth of a litre - 100 ml, musical note, round in battle, shut, together, unite, whole.

321100 合抱 hébào: encircle, joint holding, so big that one can just get one's arms around, wrap one's arm around - to describe the girth of tree trunk.

321100 因 yīn: as a result, because, by, cause, chance, comply with, conform to, connect, depend on, due,

nemonik-thinking.org

follow, for, from, go to, intimate, obey, opportunity, reason, rely on, take advantage of, then, thus.

321100 当 (當) dāng, dàng: accept, act as, adequate, appropriate, assume, at or in the very same..., bear, chime, deserve, during, equal, fitting, hold a position, in charge, in front, is, just at - time - place, knock, manage, match equally, obstruct, on the spot, ought, pawn, proper, regard as, replace, represent, right, same, should, suitable, think, to be, treat, undertake, when, withstand.

321100 走 zǒu: away, change - shape, depart, die - euphemism, form, go, go away, go by the way of, go on foot, leak, leave, let out, make a trip, meaning, move, move - vehicle, run, through, visit, walk.

321100 走马 (走馬) zǒumǎ: fine horse, gallop or trot along on horseback, on horseback, race horse, ride a horse.

321110 肖 xiāo, xiào: like, look like, resemble, seem, similar, take after.

321200 社 shè: agency, club, company, god of the soil, group, group of families, organization, society.

321200 社稷 shèjì: country, Gods of soil and grain, kingdom, state.

321201 沌 chún, dùn, tún, zhuàn: benighted, chaotic, confused, dim, first appearance Universe, murky, people without knowledge and experience, turbid, unclear, vague.

321201 沌沌 dùndùn: very unclear.

321201 祀 sì: offer libation, offer sacrifice, sacrifice, sacrifices to gods or spirits of the dead, worship.

321210 恃 shì: count, depend, mother, presume, rely, trust.

322000 佐 zuǒ: accompany, aid, aide, assist, assistant, second, subordinate.

322000 作 zuō, zuó, zuò: accomplish, act, affect, break out, busy with oneself, cause, compose, conduct, do, engage, feel, grow, make, perform to regard as, pretend, regard as, rise, show effect, take, take somebody for, use as, work, write, writings or works.

322000 匠 jiàng: artisan, carpenter, craftsman, lock-smith, manual labourer with skills, toolmaker, workman.

322000 后 (後) hòu: after, afterwards, back, behind, children, day after tomorrow, empress, last, later, queen, rear, sovereign, towards the end.

nemonik-thinking.org

322000 牡 mǔ: animal, bolt of door, hills, key, male, male - bird, or plant.

322001 色 sè, shǎi: appearance, beauty, body, colour, desire for beauty, dice, form, hue, look, sex, shade, tint.

322010 弗 fú: negative, not, without.

322100 各 gè: all, each, every, individually, respectively.

322100 名 míng: big, call, fame, famous, for people - persons, give name to, given name is, great, in the name of, influential family, lend one's name to an enterprise occasion, name, named, notable, noun - part of speech, number, own, place - e.g. among winners, position, possess, rank, renown, reputation, tell, title, titular, understand, well-known.

322100 名为 (名為) míngwèi: named as.

322100 名字 míngzi: name - e.g. what is your name, name of a person or thing.

322100 往 wǎng, wàng: back and forth, bound for - train, come and go, comes, depart, formerly, go to, leave for, past, previous, to, to and fro, to go in a direction, towards.

322100 往来 (往來) wǎnglái: back and forth, come and go, contacts, dealings, visit.

322100 环 (環) huán: bracelet, circular, encircle, go around, hem in, hoop, jade ring or bracelet, link - chain, loop, ring, ring - not for finger, scores in archery, surround.

322100 芸 (蕓) yì, yún, yùn: ability, acting, art, books and libraries, common rue - Ruta graveolens, craft, cut grass or weeds, herb used to keep insects away, imperial library, performance, rape, stunt, talent, technique, trick, weed.

322100 芸芸 yúnyún: all, diverse, every, great lot, numerous, varied.

322101 况 (況) kuàng: besides, bestow, cold water, compare, condition, elder brother, furthermore, grant, more, moreover, situation, visit.

322101 规 (規) guī: admonish, advise, compass, customs, gauge, instrument for drawing circles, law, map out, measure, overall planning, plan, regulations, rules, scheme.

322110 却 (卻) què: back, but, cool off, decline, drive back, even though, go back, however, nevertheless, retreat, step back, still, while, yet.

nemonik-thinking.org

322110 拱 gǒng: arch, arched, bow, cup one's hands in salute, encircle, fold hands in salute, fold hands on breast, join one's hands, push, salute, sprout, surround.

322110 拱璧 gǒngbì: big round jade with a hole in it, disc of jade with hole at centre, flat round jade ornament with a hole at the centre, treasure.

322200 含 hán: cherish, contain to keep, hold in mouth, keep in the mouth, suck - keep in mouth without chewing.

322200 良 liáng, liǎng: good, much, respectable, very, very much, virtuous.

322200 进 (進) jìn: admit, admonish, advance, ascend, bring, come into, dispatch, drink, eat, end, endeavour, enter, exhaust, fill, further, go into, go to court, in - into income, into - used after a verb, line of single-storey houses, make progress, money, move forward, offer, official, praise highly, present, promote, receive, recommend, score a goal, submit - present, surpass, take.

322200 进道 (進道) jìndào: access, control.

322200 进道若退 (進道若退) jìndàoruòtuì: back into the channel if, entering the Way, progress in the Dao can seem illusory, you seem to coil back.

322201 况: Mentioned in some versions, but replaced with the simplified 322101 况.

322300 图 (圖) tú: attempt, book, chart, consider again, contrive, design, diagram, drawing, expect, illustration, imitate, intentions, map, picture, plan, prepare, project, pursue, scheme, seek, tower.

323001 免 miǎn: avert, avoid, escape, evade to exempt, excuse from, excuse somebody, exempt, free somebody from something, not allowed, prohibited, remove or dismiss from office, spare.

323020 狗 gǒu: canis familiaris, dog.

323100 吹 chuī, chuì: blast, blow, boast, brag, break up, end in failure, fall through, flatter, laud to the skies, play a wind instrument, puff.

323100 径 (徑) jìng: diameter, directly, footpath, narrow path, path, straight, track, way.

323100 徒 tú: apprentice, bare, believer, companion, disciple, empty, fellow, follower, in vain, merely, no avail, on foot, only, prison sentence, simply.

nemonik-thinking.org

323100 改 gǎi: alter, alteration, amend, change, correct, improve, rectify, remodel, transform.

323100 政 zhēng, zhèng: administrative aspects of government, government, political, political affairs, politics, rule.

323210 帝 dì: creator and ruler of the Universe, emperor, god, imperialism, supreme ruler.

323300 治 chí, yí, zhì: administer, administrate, control, cure, exterminate, govern, harness - river, heal, manage, punish, regulate, research, rule, run, treat, treatment.

323300 治国 (治國) zhìguó: administer or run a country, govern, manage state affairs, rule a country.

323300 食 shí, sì, yì: animal feed, eat, eclipse, feed, food, meal.

323310 诚 (誠) chéng: certainly, earnestness, honest, indeed, real, sincerity, true.

323400 浴 yù: bath, bathe, fly up and down, shower, soak, valley, wash.

324000 所 suǒ: actual, address, grammar - passive voice, houses, institute, institutions, location, numeracy adjunct, office, particle introducing a relative clause or passive, place, small buildings, structural particle, that which.

324000 所以 suǒyǐ: as a result, hence as a result, how, reason why, so, therefore, why.

324000 所保 suǒbǎo: guarantees, place, protect, sanctuary.

324000 所居 suǒjū: dwelling, residence.

324000 所属 (所屬) suǒshǔ: affiliated, belonging to, institution, one's affiliation - i.e. the organization one is affiliated with, place, subordinate, under one's command.

324000 所谓 (所謂) suǒwèi: so called, what is called.

324101 鬼 guǐ: apparition, crafty, damnable, devil, dirty trick, ghosts, sinister design, sly, smart clever, spirit, spirit of dead, stealthy, surreptitious, underhanded.

324200 咳 hāi, hái, kài, ké: child, cough, cut off, laugh of child, remorse, separate, sound of sighing, surprise.

324200 始 shǐ: begin, establish, initiate, only then, origin, start, then.

324200 宾 (賓) bīn, bìn: discard, get rid of, guest, submit, surname, vassal, visitor.

nemonik-thinking.org

324210 逝 shì: depart, die, elapse, fades away, pass, pass away, passing of time, time flows away

324300 容 róng: allow, appearance, contain, countenance, describe, embrace, facial expression, figure, fit, for, hold, look, may be, perhaps, permit, tolerate.

325200 欮 jué: defeat, dig out, excavate, expand, fall, frustrate, hiccough, reverse, tumble, vital energy circulates in wrong direction.

325300 欲 (慾) yù: appetite, desire, greed, intend, long for, longing, lust, passion, want, wish.

325300 被 bèi, bì, pī, pì: bedding, blanket, by - marker for passive-voice sentences or clauses, cotton-padded quilt, cover, follow, framed, meet, quilt, spread, suffer, wear.

325300 资 (資) zī: ability, aid, capital, donation, expenditure, expense, funds, furnish, goods, money, natural endowment, property, provide, qualification, resources, supply, support, talent, wealth.

325300 资财 (資財) zīcái: assets, capital and goods, capital and materials, financial resources.

325310 裂 liě, liè: break, break open, crack, rend, split.

nemonik-thinking.org

326110 象 xiàng: appearance, comparable, elephant, figure, form, image, image on a map, imitate, ivory, like, mimic, of that shape, seem, shape, such as.

327001 绝 (絕) jué: absolutely, break off, by no means, cut off, cut short, definitely, disappear, discard, end, exhausted, extinct, extremely, final, most, sever, terminate, vanish.

328300 飨 (饗) xiǎng: banquet, enjoy, entertain, feast, grant, host banquet, offer food and drink, offer or enjoy sacrifice, provide dinner, receive entertainment, sacrifice, sacrificial ceremony.

328400 寥 liáo: abstruse, broad and empty, deserted, empty, few, quiet, rare, scanty, scarce, silent, uncommon, vague, deserted, empty, few, loresome, scarce, very few.

330000 古 gǔ: age-old, ancient, antiquity, archaic, books of sages, classic, old, orthodoxies of sages, paleo-, poetry.

330000 旧 (舊) jiù: ancient, bygone, former, old - opposite of new, old friend, onetime, past, used, worn with age.

330000 田 tián: arable land, cultivated, farm, field.

330000 甲 jiǎ: 1st heavenly stem, armour plating, bladed leather or metal armour, carapace, civil administration unit, first grade, first in a list as a party to a contract, nail of the fingers or toes, ranking system used in the Imperial examinations, shell, unspecified person or thing.

330000 甲兵 jiǎbīng: armour, armour-clad soldier, army force, hurt, killed, military equipment, soldier in armour, weaponry.

330000 申 shēn: 7th solar month, explain, express, extend, report, state, state - express, state to a superior, year of the Monkey.

330000 申明 shēnmíng: declare, state formally.

330100 芒 huāng, huǎng, máng, wáng: aristae of grain, awn of cereals, beard, blurred, Chinese silver-grass, cutting edge of knife or sword, distant, extensive, far away, grass - Miscanthus sinensis, indistinct, rapid, rays of light, sharp, silver-grass, sudden, tip of a blade, tip of a hair, vast, wide.

330110 帗huāng: headdress, piece of cloth or fabric to cover something, scarf, turban.

331001 亂 (乱) luàn: arbitrary, carelessly, chaos, confusion, disorder, disturbed, illicit sexual relations,

nemonik-thinking.org

indiscriminate, mix up, muddled, promiscuity, random, revolt, riot, troubled, turmoil, untidy, upheaval.

331001 克 (剋) kè, kēi: able, beat, can, capture, censure, competent, conquer, control, cut down, damage, defeat, embezzle part of what should be issued, Farmer God, forbear, gram, kill, overcome, overthrow, restrain, restrict, scold, set a time limit, seventh of the legendary Flame Emperors, subdue, surmount, transliteration.

331010 何 hé, hè: asking questions such as - what place, berate, carry, excoriate, how, how about it, let alone, needless, unnecessary, very, what, what time, when, where, which, who, why, why not.

331010 何以 héyǐ: how, how is it possible, whence, why.

331010 何故 hégù: for what reason, what for, what's the reason, why.

331010 何谓 (何謂) héwèi: what, what is meant by.

331020 制 (製) zhì: control, create, establish, make, manufacture, organisation, overpower, regulate, system.

331100 冲 (沖, 衝) chōng: according, assault, balance, break, cancel out, charge, clash, collide, dash against - water, dash onward, deep, develop, develop - film, dynamic, empty, face, flatland, flush, forceful, full of vigour and drive, give offense, great force, highway, humble, immature, important place, in view of, infuse, irritating the nose, mix with water, opposition, pour, powerful, public road, punch, pungent, rinse, rise in the air, rush forward, shoot up, soar, straight ahead, strong - smell, surge up, thoroughfare, touch, towards, vigorous, war carriage, wash out, water, without worldly desires.

331100 坚 (堅) jiān: armour, firm, fortification, hard, heavily fortified point, resolute, solid - ice, steadfast, strong, stronghold.

331100 坚强 (堅強) jiānqiáng: staunch, strong.

331100 曳 yè, yì: drag, haul, pull, tow, trail, tug.

331100 民 mín: citizen, nationality, people, subjects.

331100 足 jù, zú: adequate, ample, as much as, attain, enough, foot, footprint, satisfy, sufficient.

331100 足下 (敢為) zúxià: below the foot, you, you - used to a superior or between persons of the same generation.

331100 足以 zúyǐ: enough, so much so that, so that, sufficient.

331200 武 wǔ: martial, military, valiant, warlike.

331200 冲: Mentioned in some versions, but replaced with the simplified 331100 冲.

331201 思 sī: consider, final particle, hope, miss, ponder, think, thought.

332000 伯 bà, bǎi, bó: earl, eldest brother, father's elder brother, feudal rank - Count, older brother, one hundred, paternal elder uncle, respectful form of address, senior, senior male - Sire, third of five orders of nobility, uncle.

332000 听 (聽) tīng, tìng, yín: allow, can - canned beverages, comply, hear, let, listen, obey, supervise, tin, understand.

332001 现 xiàn: appear, become visible, manifest.

332010 狎 xiá: disrespect, familiar, hazard, intimate, no respect, take by force.

332100 使 shǐ, shì: ambassador, apply, arrange, cause, dispatch, employ, enable, envoy, exercise, instruct, lead, let, make, message, messenger, mission, order, send on a mission, use.

332100 和 hé, hè, huó, huò: and, blend, calm, cap a poem, complete a set in mah-jong or playing cards, compose poem, draw, friendly, gentle, good terms, harmony, join in the singing, kind, mild, mix powder and water, mix together, peace, peaceful, respond in singing, soft, sum, tie, to, together, tranquil, union, warm, with.

332100 怕 pà: afraid, apprehensive, dread, fear, may be, perhaps, scared, suppose, unable to bear, unable to endure.

332101 虺 huī, huǐ: large poisonous snake, lizard, mythical venomous snake, sick, venomous snake or viper, with no ambition.

332200 咎 jiù, gāo: blame, calamity, catastrophe, censure, defect, error, fault, fearful, fierce, misfortune, mistake, offence, punish, reproach, terrible.

332200 或 huò, yù: either, else, may be, might, occasionally, or, perhaps, possibly, probably, puzzle, remotely, some, someone, sometimes.

332200 莅 (涖) lì: administer, approach - administrator, arrive, at present, attend - official function, be present, come, manage, reach, rule, watch.

332200 识 (識) shí, shì, zhì: know, knowledge, recognize, record, understand, write a footnote.

332211 阅 (閱, 閲) yuè: examine, experience, go over, go through, inspect, look over, pass through, peruse, read, review.

332300 浊 (濁) zhuó: deep and rough voice, dirty, filthy, impure, muddy, turbid.

332300 蚤 zǎo, zhǎo: early, early morning, flea, fortunately, louse, luckily.

332310 惊 (驚) jīng: alarm, distress, frightened, scared, shy, start, startle, surprise, upset.

333100 荣 (榮) róng: bloom, flourish, flower, glory, grow luxuriantly, honour, parasol, prosper, thrive, throw, upturned eaves.

333200 哀 āi: beg, bemoan, bewail, care, cherish, condole, desolate, distressed, doleful, farmer God, grief, lament, mercy, mood, mourn, pity, reluctant, sad, sixth of legendary Flame Emperors, solicitude, sorrow, supplicate, sympathy.

333200 涉 dié, shè: concern, enter, experience, ford stream, go through, involved, little knowledge, travel across ocean, wade across.

333200 积 (積) jī: accumulate, achievement, add up, amass, habitual, hold in store, indigestion, integrate -

nemonik thinking.org

math, latent, long-standing, measured quantity, merit, old, product - multiplication, solve - math, stagnate, store up, wrinkled clothing.

333200 积德 (積德) jīdé: accumulate merit, do good, give to charity, good deeds, virtuous actions.

333201 说 (說) shuì, shuō, tuō, yuè: canvass, criticize, doctrine, explain, persuade, persuasive speaker, say, scold, speak, talk, teachings, tell off, theory, upbraid.

333300 涉 dié, shè: cross - river, ford stream, go through, involve, wade.

333300 甾 zāi, zī: calamity, disaster, evil, ground that has been cultivated for one year, jar for wine, pheasant, pottery, steroid, steroid nucleus.

333300 粪 (糞) fèn, sān: dung, excrement, manure, night soil, shit.

333300 贼 (賊) zé, zéi: deceitful, especially, evil, extremely, kill, thief, traitor, wily.

333310 离 (離) chī, lí, lì: away from, depart, elegant, far away, from - giving distances, go away, independent, leave, mythical beast, one of the Eight Trigrams symbolizing fire, part from, rare beast, separate, separate, strange, without.

nemonik-thinking.org

333401 惑 huò: baffle, bewildered, confuse, doubt, mislead, perplexed, puzzled, uncertain.

334101 虚 (虛) qū, xū: abstract theory or guiding principles, devoid of content, diffident, empty, false, humble or modest, in vain, no avail, timid, unoccupied, virtual, waste, weak – health.

334101 虚言 (虛言) xūyán: bubble, empty words, false words, unreal words.

334201 税 (稅) shuì, tuàn, tuì, tuō: duties, tax.

334201 蛇 chí, shé, tuó, yí: serpent, snake.

334210 稀 xī: diluted, few, rare, scarce, seldom, sparse, uncommon, unusual, watery.

334300 奥 (奧) ào: abstruse, difficult to understand, mysterious, obscure, profound, secret corner house.

335000 绁 (紲) xiè, yì: bind, bundle, contract, draw in, exceed, fasten, hold on a leash, leash, overstep, reduce, rein, rope, shorten, tie.

335000 细 (細) xì: careful, close, delicate, detailed, exquisite, fine, fine silk, finely particulate, frugal, humble, insignificant, little, meticulous, minute, quiet - sound, sharp, shrill, slender, small, small crime, small

nemonik-thinking.org

particles, soft, soft and high pitched, tender, thin, tiny, trifling, trivial, young.

335201 疏 shū, shù: alienated, annotation, careless, clear away obstruction, commentary, detach, distant - relation, dredge, drift apart, estranged, keep at arm's length, lax, neglect, negligent, not close, not familiar, overlook, present a memorial to the Emperor, scanty, scatter, sparse, thin.

335210 累 (纍) léi, lěi, lèi, lù: accumulate, bind together, bother, bull, continuous, copulate, cord, cumbersome, exhaust, fatigue, implicate, involve, lay on top, pile up, repeated, rope, running, strain, tired, toil, truss up, twist around, wear out, weary, work hard.

335210 累累 léiléi: accumulated, again and again, clusters, countless, dejected, disappointed, exhausted, heaps, innumerable, piles of, repeated, riddled with, tired, wretched.

335300 細: Mentioned in some versions, but replaced with the simplified 335000 细.

335310 弊 bì: abuse, bad, corrupt, criminal, defeat, detriment, disadvantage, evil, fraud, harm, irregular, malpractice, shortcoming, wrong.

337400 谬 (謬) miù: absurd, cheat, confuse, deceive, empty, erroneous, error, exaggeration, false, falsehood, mistake, void, wrong.

338201 歔 xū: blow, blow through nose, exhale from nose, heave a sigh, snort.

340000 曲 qū, qǔ: bend, bent, crooked, curving, false, let something bend, opposite of straight, river with curve, song, tune, wrong.

340001 岂 (豈) kǎi, qǐ: how, how can it be that, what.

341010 荆 (荊) jīng: bramble, cane, chaste tree or berry - Vitex agnus-castus, difficulty, thorns, wife.

341010 荆棘 (荊棘) jīngjí: brambles, thistles and thorns, thorny undergrowth.

341011 剋: Mentioned in some versions, but replaced with the simplified 331001 克.

341100 员 (員) yuán, yún, yùn: able general, employee, hairdresser, increase, member, numerous, person, person engaged in some field of activity - cook - teacher etc., personnel, revolve, rotate, spin, staff member, student.

341100 员员 (員員) yuányuán: very numerous.

nemonik-thinking.org

341101 荒 huāng, huǎng, kāng: absurd, barren, crop failure, crude, desert, desolate, dissolute, famine, fantastic, neglect, out of practice, out of practice, roughly processed, scarce, scarcity, self-indulgent, short, shortage, shortage, uncultivated land, waste, wasteland.

341110 尚 shàng: esteem, even, fairly, lay stress on, pay great attention, rather, respect, set great store by, still, value, yet.

341210 闽 (閩) mǐn: river, tribe.

342100 保 bǎo: bail, defend, ensure, guarantee, guarantor, guard, hold, insure, keep, last, maintain, protect, safeguard.

342100 保管员 bǎoguǎnyuán: custodian, storeroom clerk.

342100 恬 tián: calm, carefree, peaceful, quiet, tranquil, uncaring, unperturbed.

342100 恬淡 tiándàn: content, dispassionate, do not seek benefit or merit, indifferent to fame or gain, no desire, no interest, quiet.

342200 战 (戰) zhàn: attack, battle, combat fight, shiver, shudder, tremble, war.

nemonik-thinking.org

342200 战胜 (戰勝) zhànshèng: defeat, overcome, prevail, surmount, vanquish.

342200 益 yì: add, advantage, all the more, beneficial, benefit, increase, profit.

343100 徙 xǐ: change one's residence, migrate, move, move one's abode, remove, shift.

344100 倾 (傾) qīng: admire, bend, collapse, decay, deviation, discord, do all one can, empty, exhaust, incline, lean, overflow, overturn, pour out, surpass, tend, tendency, upset, use up all one's resources.

344300 婴 (嬰) yīng: baby, bother, infant.

344300 婴儿 (嬰兒) yīng'ér: baby, if, infancy, infant, leading, to.

344310 蔽 bì, fù: block, conceal, cover, curtain on both sides of hearse - dead wagon, hide, meat wagon, screen, shelter, shield, spread over.

349300 缨 (纓) yīng: annoy, bother, cap or hat ribbon, chin strap, coloured ribbon, leather ribbon, ribbon, shaped like a tassel - leaf etc., strap, suffer, tassel - hat, twine.

351010 拙 zhuō: awkward, clumsy, convention, crude, dull, inelegant, my, stupid.

nemonik-thinking.org

351100 临 (臨) lín, lìn: about, approach, arrive, copy, descend face, draw near, face, facing, just about to, just before, labour, overlook, presence, reach.

352010 带 (帶) dài: and, area, band, bear - i.e. to have, belt, bring, bring up, carry, consists of, contain, drive spur on, girdle, have, lace, lead, lead to action, look after, raise, region, ribbon, show, strap, take, take along, tape, tire, wear, with, zone.

352201 慌 huāng, huǎng: abandon, absurd, afraid, awfully, confused, crop, debauchery, desolate, dim, dread, failure, famine, fantastic, fear, flee, flurried, flustered, frantic, hurried, indistinct, lean year, lie, lose one's head, ludicrous, neglect, nervous, panicky, ridiculous, scarcity, scared, shortage, unbearable, waste.

354310 幤: Mentioned in some versions, but replaced with the simplified 121010 币.

361100 监 (監) jiān: control, direct, firm, hard, inspect, inspector, jail, prison, solid, strong, supervise, supervisor.

361100 诎 (詘) qū, qù: be over, bend, bow, complete, crook, crouch, curved, demote, exhausted, humiliate, lack, mute, oust, relegate, shorten, stoop, stutter, suddenly, wrong, yield.

365400 懷 huái: carry in the bosom or the sleeve, conceal, wrap.

400000

401110 寿 (壽) shòu: age, birthday, burial, funerary, life, lifespan, live, long life, longevity, old age.

402110 夸 (誇) kuā: boast, exaggerated, extravagant, handsome, head, leader, luxurious, overstate, praise.

403110 抟 (摶) tuán, zhuān: circle, knead, model, roll around with hand, spiral.

404310 寂 jì: desolate, lonely, lonesome, quiet, silent, solitary, still.

404310 寂寥 jìliáo: desolate, lonely, lonesome, solitary, still.

404310 旁 bàng, páng: assist, beside, broad, by side, close, depend, else, extensive, follow, great, near, nearby, one side, other, round, self, side, transverse.

404410 祭 jì, zhài: festive occasion, memorial service, sacrifice, wield, worship.

404410 祭祀 jìsì: offer sacrifices to gods or ancestors., sacrifice.

nemonik-thinking.org

404410 祭祭 jìjì: extreme sacrifice, sacrifice.

406310 朘 juān, zuī: contract, decrease, deprive, exploit, male organ, man's genital, reduce, wane.

410110 寻 (尋) xín, xún: ancient, continuously, endless, long time, look for, no stop, search, seek, unclear.

410110 寻寻 xúnxún: continuously, endless, infinite, long time, look for, no stop, search, seek, unclear, unlimited.

411010 有 yǒu, yòu: appear, be, being, comparison, estimate, exist, existence, happen, has, have, is, keep, opposite of 无 Non-existence, own, possess, substance, there are, there is, what is, will be.

411010 有为 (有為) yǒuwéi: promising, show promise.

411010 有余 (有餘) yǒuyú: abundance, enough and to spare, odd, surplus.

411010 有力 yǒulì: energetic, forceful, powerful, strong, vigorous.

411010 有名 yǒumíng: celebrated, defined, described, famous, known, named, noted, renowned, well-known.

411010 有志 yǒuzhì: a wilful man will have his way, ambitious, everyone has his own ambition, interested, where there's a will there's a way.

411010 有所 yǒusuǒ: somewhat, to some extent.

411010 有无 (有無) yǒuwú: corporeal and incorporeal, have or have not, something may or may not exist, surplus and shortfall, tangible and intangible, there is the former but not the latter, with the former there is no need for the latter.

411010 有益 yǒuyì: advantageous, beneficial, good for, profitable, useful, valuable.

411010 有罪 yǒuzuì: culpability, guilty.

411010 有请 (有請) yǒuqǐng: ask a visitor in, ask somebody in, ask somebody to do something - e.g. make a speech, request the pleasure of seeing somebody.

411010 有道 yǒudào: accomplished in the Way, adhere to the principles of truth and right, good government prevails, have attained the Way, lawful, learned and virtuous, reasonable, right.

411120 持 chí: accumulate, control, direct, grasp, hold, keep, maintain, manage, oppose, persevere, run - administer, support, sustain.

411300 注 (註) zhòu, zhù: annotation, centralise, comment, concentrate, direct, focus, focus attention, gaze, inject, notes, pay attention, pour into, record, register, stake - gambling, sums of money, watch attentively.

412000 刍 (芻) chú: cut grass, fodder, grass, hay, mow or cut grass, straw.

412010 争 (爭) zhēng, zhèng: argue, compete, contend, debate, deficient, dispute, fight, how, lacking, quarrel, strive, struggle, vie for, what.

412010 孝 xiào: filial, filial piety, mourning, mourning apparel, obedience.

412010 身 juān, shēn, yuán: body, character, clothes, conduct, hull, in person, life, main part of a structure or body, morality, oneself, person, personally, pregnant, status, suit, themselves, torso, trunk, twinset, yourself.

412010 身为 (身為) shēnwéi: as, in the capacity of.

412010 身后 (身後) shēnhòu: after one's death, behind the body, one's social background, posthumous.

412010 邦 bāng: country, nation, state.

412010 邦家 bāngjiā: country, nation, state.

412020 阴 (陰) ān, yīn, yìn: back, cloudy, concave, dark, female principle, feminine, genitalia, hidden, implicit, insidious, lunar, moon, negative, north side of mountain, opposite of Yang, overcast, secret, secret,

nemonik-thinking.org

shady, sinister, south side of river, spirit world, Yin - negative principle of Yin and Yang.

412021 抱 bào: adopt, carry in arms, cherish, embrace, enfold, harbour, hold or carry in the arm, hug, join together, surround, unite.

412100 夆 féng, páng: butt as horned animals, resist.

412110 夷 yí: arrogant, barbarian, capture, damaged or killed without a mark, demolish, exterminate, flat, foreign country, foreigner, gentle, happy, hesitate, joyful, kill, leisurely, level to the ground, modest, peace, peaceful, put to death, raze, root out, ruin, safe, same kind, smooth, tear down, usual, wipe out, wounded.

412200 宝 (寶) bǎo: antique, gambling device, gem, jewel, precious, precious, rare, treasure, treasure, treasured, valuable, valuable, value, your esteemed.

412200 美 měi: beautiful, delicious, elated, exulting, fair, fine, good, good deed, good-looking, handsome, ideal, nice, pleased with oneself, pleasing, praise, pretty, satisfactory, someone, something that satisfies.

412210 育 yō, yù: bring up, educate, education, give birth, have children, nourish, produce, raise, rear.

412220 鸡 (雞) jī: chicken, cock, fowl, hen.

memonik-thinking.org

412300 泽 (澤) duó, shì, yì, zé: beneficence, brilliance, damp, favour, grace, kindness, lustre - metals marsh, moist, pond, pool, radiance, sheen, swamp.

413000 军 (軍) jūn: arms, army, forces, military, regiment, soldiers, troops.

413010 角 jiǎo, jué, gǔ, lù: ancient three legged wine vessel, angle, compete, corner, horn, horn-shaped, musical note, point, role - theatre, unit of money - 0.1 yuan.

413100 侯 hóu, hòu: lord, marquis, nobleman or high official, second of the five orders of ancient Chinese nobility, target in archery.

413100 层 (層) céng: floor - building, laminated, layers, repeated, sheaf math, step, story - building, stratum.

413210 侮 wǔ: disgrace, humiliate, insult, ridicule.

413210 辱 rǔ, rù: abuse, bring disgrace or humiliation, disgrace, dishonour, humiliate, indebted, insult, self-deprecating, shame.

413300 宰 zǎi: butcher, cheat customers, control, dictate, dominate, exploit, govern, imperial official, in charge of, master, official, oppress, responsible, rule, slaughter, slaughter livestock, trample underfoot.

nemonik-thinking.org

414120 弥 (彌, 瀰) mí: brimming, broad, complete, cover, distant, extensive, fill up, fix up, full, long, more, overflowing, put down, relax bow, spread out, stop.

414200 室 shì: chamber, family or clan, grave, home, house, one of the 28 constellations, room, scabbard, work unit.

414201 梡 hún, kuǎn: ancient four-legged sacrificial table, sacrifice, stand for sacrifice, tray for carrying sacrificial meat, tree.

414300 凌 líng: approach, bully, encroach, ice, insult, maltreat, pure, rise high, soar, thick ice, virtuous.

414310 新 xīn: fresh, meso- - chemistry, modern, new, newly, recently.

414400 筮 shì: divination, divination with stalks of plants, divining rod.

415110 教 jiāo, jiào: ask, cause, class, education, instruct, make, order, religion, teaching, tell.

415110 教父 jiàofù: godfather.

415310 傍 bàng, páng: approaching, approaching, around, beside, close, depend on, draw near, intimate relationship, near, nestle, other, side.

nemonik-thinking.org

415800 飙 (飆) biāo: hurricane, quick, rapid, storm, stormy gale, swift, violent storm wind, violent wind, whirlwind, wind.

420000 且 jū, qiě: about, also - post-subject, and, both, but also, for a long time to come, for the time being, further, in addition, moreover, when, will soon - pre-verb, yet.

420000 目 mù: catalogue, division, eye, goal, item, list, look, name, order - taxonomy, section, see, table of contents, title, topic.

420000 目明 mùmíng: sharp sighted.

420000 目盲 mùmáng: blind, blindness.

420010 司 sī: company, control, department - ministry, direct, in charge, manage, officer, operate, preside, run, stand for, take charge, uphold.

420110 时 (時) shí: age, era, fashion, grammar -tense, hour, o'clock, opportunity, period, season, tense - past, time, when.

420110 甫 fǔ, pǔ, pù: begin, distance of ten li, father, father - euphemism, great, just, just now, man, man's courtesy name, only.

421000 弄 lòng, nòng: alley, do, fetch, fiddle with, fix, fool with, get, handle, lane, make, manage, mess with, play, toy with.

421000 百 bǎi, bó, mò: all kinds of, hundred, many, numerous, one hundred.

421000 百倍 bǎibèi: hundred fold, hundred times, rise - social status - price, rise sharply.

421000 百姓 bǎishēng, bǎishěng: common people.

421000 百姓 bǎixìng: common people.

421000 百谷 (百穀) bǎigǔ: all kind of grains, every kind of cereal crop.

421000 自 zì: from, naturally, oneself, personal, private, self, since, themselves, thing.

421000 自为 (自為) zìwéi: each acts on his own will, for oneself, lack of coordination, since the.

421000 自古 zìgǔ: from time immemorial, since ancient times, since antiquity.

421000 自各 zìgě: oneself, since the.

421000 自大 zìdà: arrogant.

421000 自是 zìshì: consider oneself always in the right, naturally, of course, opinionated, regard oneself as infallible.

nemonik-thinking.org

421000 自来 (自來) zìlái: always, come of one's own accord, from the beginning, in the first place, originally.

421000 自然 zìrán: expected, natural, naturally, nature, without forethought.

421000 自然之道 zìránzhīdào: nature's way, way of nature.

421000 自然德 zìrándé: natural virtue.

421000 自爱 (自愛) zì'ài: cherish one's good name, regard for oneself, self-love, self-regard, self-respect, take good care of one's health.

421000 自称 (自稱) zìchēng: call oneself, claim a title, claim to be, declare oneself to be, profess.

421000 自视 (自視) zìshì: consider - think - imagine oneself, view oneself.

421001 酉 yǒu: 10th earthly branch, 10th terrestrial branch, cock, hen, mature, old, pond, tenth of the twelve Earthly branches, unitary, wine, wine vessel.

421010 号 (號) háo, hào: assumed name, bugle call, business establishment, cry, day of a month, horn - wind instrument, howl, mark, number - ordinal, number of people, roar, sign, size, suffix used after name of a ship, symbol, take a pulse, yell.

nemonik-thinking.org

421100 其 jī, qí: he, her, him, his, it, its, she, such, that, their, them, these, they, this, those.

421100 其一 qíyī: first, firstly, one of the given options.

421100 其中 qízhōng: among which - them etc., in the midst of them - it - that, in which - it etc., included among these, inside.

421100 其后 (其後) qíhòu: after, after that, afterwards, later, next.

421100 其妙 jīmiào: intriguing, marvellous, unable to make head or tail of something, wonderful.

421100 其实 (其實) qíshí: actually, in fact, really.

421100 其所 qísuǒ: all be properly placed and provided for, cater to another's pleasure, die a worth death, each has a role to play, forget oneself, hit on what somebody likes, it, its place, one's appointed place, pander to somebody's whims, place, the place for that, to the best of one's ability.

421100 其次 qícì: next, secondary, secondly.

421100 其言 qíyán: break one's promise, listen to what a person says and watch what he does, take note of somebody's words but judge him by his deeds, their words.

421100 其身 qíshēn: if he, themselves.

421100 旷 (曠) kuàng: broad, desert, empty, extensive, open, skip, spacious, vacant, vast, waste, wide, wilderness.

421100 枉 wǎng: askew, bend, bent, crooked, curving, distort, futile, in the wrong, in vain, misrepresent, no purpose, treat unjustly, twist, useless, wrong.

421110 亨 hēng, pēng, xiǎng: enjoy, no trouble progressing, prosperous, smoothly, unit of inductance – henry.

421110 奇 jī, qí: abnormal, occult, odd, odd number, rare, remarkable, strange, surprise, uncanny, unexpected, unusual, weird, wonderful.

421110 奇事 qíshì: a wonder, marvel, strange affair, unusual phenomenon.

421110 讳 (諱) huì: avoid, conceal, die, fear, forbidden word, name of deceased emperor or superior, shun, taboo.

421120 俞 shù, yú: accede, approve, assent, consent, increase, make boat by hollowing the log, more, OK, permit, pleasant, promise, stable, yes used by Emperor.

nemonik-thinking.org

421120 前 qián: ago, ahead, before, earlier, first, former, formerly, forward, front, future, in front, preceding, previous.

421120 前后 (前後) qiánhòu: about, all around, altogether, around, around the time of, back and forth, before and after, from beginning to end, from start to finish, front and rear.

422100 取 qǔ: accept, associate, choose, court, fetch, get, invite, obtain, position, receive, select to take, take.

422100 知 zhī, zhì: aware, comprehend, know, knowledge, perceive, recognise, remember, understand.

422100 知有 zhīyǒu: known each other long, known to have.

422100 知足 zhīzú: content, content with one's lot, content with one's situation, contentment, happiness, know when it is enough.

422110 拾 jiè, shè, shí: collate or arrange, collect, pick up, ten, ten (banker's anti-fraud numeral), tidy up.

422200 泊 bó, pō, pó, pò: anchor - vessel, at anchor, berth, boat, earl, eldest, lake, lie at anchor, moor-boat, not seek fame and wealth, poise, quiet, stay, stop over, thin, touch, uncle, white water.

nemonik-thinking.org

422300 祥 xiáng: advantage, auspicious, fortune, good luck, good omen, happiness, lucky, propitious.

422321 愈 (癒) yù: better, even more, heal, more, more and more, recover, recover from illness, the more.

422410 烹 pēng: boil, boil alive - capital punishment, cook, cooking method, cuisine, quick fry, stir fry.

423010 易 yì: amiable, change, easy, exchange, replace, simple, transform.

423101 聋 (聾) lóng: deaf.

423110 张 (張) zhāng: exaggerate, expand, extend, flat objects, inflate, lay on, look, open, open up, sheet - paper, spread, spread out, stretch, unfold, votes.

423200 殃 yāng: calamity, disaster, misfortune.

423201 眺 tiào: gaze afar, gaze at, look at, look into distance, scan, survey.

423210 宵 xiāo: all night, dark, evening, night, root of grass, weed.

423310 策 cè: bamboo slip for writing, encourage, essay, method, plan, policy, riding crop with sharp spines, scheme, spur, strategy, suggestion, upward horizontal stroke in calligraphy, urge, whip – horse.

423400 寒 hán: afraid, chilly, cold, poor, tremble, wintry.

424011 驷 (駟) sì: horses, team of four horses.

424110 降 jiàng, xiáng, xiàng: capitulate, come down, cut down, decrease, descend, detract, down, drop, fall, lower, reduce, showdown, sink, subdue, surrender, tame, vanquish.

424111 猶: Mentioned in some versions, but replaced with the simplified 103111 犹.

424200 客 kè: customer, guest, traveller, visitor.

424200 殆 dài: almost, danger, dangerous, endanger, only, perilous, probably.

424210 陵 líng: hills, hilly, mausoleum, mound, mountain, tomb.

424211 袌 bào: carry, carry in the arms, embrace, front of robe or jacket, gown, hold.

424300 涣 (渙) huàn: demoralised, disperse, dissipate, expansive - river, sap, scatter, someone who was misunderstood or suspected, very wide moving water like a sea.

424300 释 (釋) shì, yì: cheerful, clear up, dispel, elucidate, explain, happy, interpret, joyous, let go, release, relieved, set free.

nemonik-thinking.org

425101 毫 háo: at all, dime, drawing brush, extremely small, fine long hair, in the least, little, long hair, measure of length, millimetre, one thousandth, tip of a hair, unit of length, unit of weight - 0.005 grams, whit, writing brush.

425101 毫末 háomò: ends of long fine hairs, extremely small, small shoot of tree, tip of hair.

425301 窥 (窺) ku, kuǐ: look, peep, pry about, secretly watch, spy, watch.

430000 吉 jí: auspicious, fortunate, giga - billion or 10^9, good, lucky, propitious.

430000 早 zǎo: early, good morning, long ago, morning, soon.

430000 早已 zǎoyǐ: already, die, for long time, in the past, long ago, perish.

430010 同 tóng, tòng: alike, like, merge, same, similar, together, unification, with.

430010 同一 tóngyī: identical, same, unanimous.

430110 间 (間) jiān, jiàn: among, between, divide, gap, interstice, locality, midpoint, opening, place, room, section of a room or lateral space between two pairs of pillars, separate, sow discontent, sow discord, space

nemonik-thinking.org

between, thin out - seedlings, within, within a definite time or space.

431000 但 dàn: but, however, merely, only, still, yet.

431000 佳 jiā: auspicious, beautiful, delightful, excellent, fine, good, good news, satisfy.

431000 声 (聲) shēng: announce, declare, fame, music, noise, reputable, reputation, sound, tone, voice.

431000 声人 (聲人) shēngrén: reputable person.

431010 阳 (陽) yáng: light, male principle - Taoism, open, opposite of Yin, overt, positive - electric, sun, sunlight, sunny side of the mountain, Yang.

431020 阿 ā, ē: bent, big mound, cater for, corner, dad, elder brother, eldest, final particle, flatter, graceful, initial particle, interjection, kinship terms to indicate familiarity, little sister, pander, partial, play up, prefix used before monosyllabic names.

431100 单 (單) chán, dān, shàn: alone, bill, chief, chieftain, encircle, form, individual, list, lone, odd number, one, only, revolve, sheet, simple, single, solely, solitary, surround, thin, unlined - clothing, weak.

nemonik-thinking.org

431100 启 (啟, 啓) qǐ: awaken, begin, commence, enlighten, explain, inform, initiate, open, Qi son of Yu the Great - founder Xia Dynasty, start, state.

431100 味 wèi: flavour, savour, smell, taste.

431100 果 guǒ, kè, luǒ, wǒ: achieve, consequence, decisive, fruit, if really, indeed, just as expected or stated, outcome, resolute, result, succeed.

431100 舍 (捨) shě, shè, shì: abandon, abolish, altruistic, arrange residence, barracks, discard, dormitory, dwelling, give, give alms, give up, give up willingly, house, hut, inn, launch, my, part with, put, put aside, put something in place, put up, remit, reside, residence, rest, shed, son of a feudal prince or high official, stop, take up quarters, tavern, unit of distance equal to 30 li, young master of the house.

431100 责 (責) zé, zhài: ask reprovingly, blame, demand, duty, entrust, obligate, one's responsibility, reproach, require, responsibility.

431110 即 jí: approach, ascend throne, assume office, at once, at present, be, come into contact, draw near, even if, i.e., immediately, meaning, namely, near, present - time, prompt, prompted by occasion, promptly, quickly, reach, right away, same, that is, undertake.

431110 命 mìng: appoint, assign a name – named - call, call, command, destiny, fate, fortune, instruction, life, lifespan, lot, luck, named, order or commanc, title.

431110 诃 (訶, 呵) hē: abuse, blame, curse, rebuke, ridicule in loud voice, scold loudly.

431110 闻 (聞) wén, wèn: fame, famous, hear, heard before, listen, make known, news, reputation, smell, sniff at, something has been heard, well-known.

431110 闻名 (聞名) wénmíng: eminent, famous, renowned, well-known.

431210 河上公 Heshanggong: Chinese philosopher He-Shang Gong (179-157 BC), version of Lao Zi's Dao De Jing.

432000 卑 bēi: base, despise, humble, inferior, low, modest, vulgar.

432000 垢 gòu: dirt, disgrace, filth, shame.

432001 昆 hùn, kūn: after, bright, children, descendant, elder brother, insect, many, offspring, poetry, progeny, together, undivided.

nemonik-thinking.org

432010 耶 yē, yé: interrogative particle, final particle interrogative particle, used in transliteration, yeah.

432100 便 biàn, pián: advantage, cheap, convenient, defecate, ease, even if, excretion, expedient, handy, in that case, informal, ordinary, plain, relieve oneself, simple, so, soon afterwards, then, thus, urinate, when the chance arises.

432100 备 (備) bèi: against, equipment, have, make up the number, perfect, perform garrison duty, prepare, provide, ready, simply fill the post, store, utmost.

432100 姑 gū: aunt, father's sister, for the time being - literary, husband's mother, husband's sister, nun, paternal aunt, sister in law, temporary.

432100 故 gù: ancient, because, cause, dead, deceased, die, former, friend, happening, hence, incident, instance, intentional, old, old friend, pass away, previous, purposely, reason, therefore.

432100 故人 gùrén: former spouse, friend, old friend.

432100 故去 gùqù: death, die, pass away.

432100 故居 gùjū: former dwelling, former home, former residence.

432100 故常 gùcháng: constant.

nemonik-thinking.org

432100 故杀 gùshā: intentional homicide, premeditated murder, wilful murder.

432100 故称 (故稱) gùchēng: it said, obsolete word, old term.

432100 故道 gùdào: old method, old road, old way.

432100 畋 tián: cultivate land, field, hunt, till land.

432100 眇 miǎo, miào: blind, blind in one eye, detail, humble, little, minuscule, minute, negligible, paltry, people with one eye, small, stare, subtle, tiny, very small.

432110 倚 yǐ: depend, lean against, lean heavily lean on, rely on.

432110 虿 (蠆) chài: insect, kind of scorpion.

432120 偷 tōu: burglar, drift along, manage to make, pilfer, secretly, snatch, steal, stealthily, thief.

432200 倍 bèi: double, increase, multiple times - two fold - three fold etc., multiply, times - multiplier, twice.

432200 兼 jiān: and, annex, combine, concurrently, connect, double, have both, holding two or more official posts at the same time, merge, simultaneous, twice, unite.

432200 惟 wéi: but, however, -ism, nevertheless, only.

nemonik-thinking.org

432400 黑 hè, hēi: black, blackboard, dark, evil, gangland, secret, sinister, wicked.

433001 皆 jiē: all of, each and every, every, everybody, everyone, in all cases.

433001 皆知 jiēzhī: all knows, everyone knows, known, known to all, public knowledge.

433100 敌 (敵) dí: enemy, equal, foe, hold back, match, oppose, resist, rival, withstand.

433110 脩 tiáo, xiū: build, construct, cultivate, decorate, dried meat - teachers payment, edit, embellish, fine food, follow, good, manage, mend, numeration private tutor, repair, self-cultivate, study, teacher's pay, trim.

433200 根 gēn: base, based on, basis, cause, foot, foundation, long slender objects, origin, radical - chemistry, root.

433200 格 gē, gé: arrive, case - legal, character, check, come, division, fight, form, frame, grid, gurgle, hinder, impede, investigate, lattice, obstruct, pattern, probe into, rattle, resist, rule, shape, square, standard, study carefully, study exhaustively, style.

433200 载 (載) zǎi, zài: also, and, as well as, carry, convey, fill up, filled, hold, load, one year, put on record, record in writing, simultaneously, transport, while, write down, year.

433210 崇 chóng: dignified, esteem, high, honour, lofty, revere, sublime, think highly, venerate, worship.

433300 業: Mentioned in some versions, but replaced with the simplified 121100 业.

433300 退 tuì: backward, cancel, fade, quit, recede, resign, retreat, return, step back, withdraw, decline, move back, retreat, step back, withdraw.

433300 鉴 (鑑, 鋻) jiàn: bronze mirror, example, inspect, letter, looking glass, mirror, reflection, something can be warning, view, warn, watch carefully.

433400 蒞: Mentioned in some versions, but replaced with the simplified 332200 莅.

433410 满 (滿) mǎn, mèn: complete, contented, fill to brim, fulfil, full, fully, packed, quite, reach the limit, satisfied.

433410 满堂 (滿堂) mǎntáng: all booked up, all those present, entire audience, filled, have a full house, jam-packed, packed, sell-out - capacity audience, whole audience, whole house.

434000 饵 (餌) ěr: allure, bait, biscuit, bread, cake, dumplings, entice, food, lure, pastry, swallow, tempt.

434100 顽 (頑) wán: die-hard, have no knowledge, incorrigible, mischievous, naughty, obstinate, opinionated, pig-headed, play, recalcitrant, stubborn, stupid.

434200 畜 chù, xù: domestic animal, livestock, raise - animals, rear.

434300 楚 chǔ: ancient place name, bush, bush used in Chinese medicine - genus Vitex, clear, distinct, orderly, pain, punishment cane, suffering.

435000 结 (結) jì, jiē, jié: bear - fruit, bind, bond, cement, check out - hotel, coagulate, conclude, congeal, connect, fasten, firm, forge, form - seed, freeze, gather together, join, junction, knit, knot, node, produce, results, settle, solid, sturdy, tie, unite, weave, written undertaking.

435000 结者 (結者) jiézhě: weave, weaver.

440000 臣 chén: address when speaking to a ruler, bureaucracy, control, courtier, minister, official, people between ruler and common people, serve a ruler as his subject, state official or subject in dynastic China, statesman, submit to the rule of or acknowledge allegiance, vassal, your servant.

440010 苛 hē, hé, kē: exacting, harsh, petty, rigorous, severe, small.

440110 闸 (閘) zhá: block, brake, canal lock, dam, electric switch or circuit breaker, flood gate, gear, lock on waterway, sluice, sluice gate, switch, water-gate.

441000 若 ré, rě, rè, ruò: according, arrive, as, as if, assuming, choose, compliance, equal, handle, if, in case, just like, like, match, obedient, promise, seem, similar, such as, supposing, treat, trim vegetables, you.

441000 若何 ruòhè: how, how then, what, what then.

441001 兕 sì: female rhinoceros, rhinoceros indicus.

441010 孟 mèng: eldest, eldest brother, eminent, first in series, first month of a season, great.

441010 苟 gōu, gǒu: but, careless, casual, distinguish, frivolous, grass name, greedy, humble, if, if indeed, if only, illicit, indifferent, negligent, particle - if, provided, temporarily, thoughtless.

441010 陆 (陸) liù, lù: army, continent, continental, land, shore, six - banker's anti-fraud numeral, six on cheques.

mnemonik-thinking.org

441100 枯 kū: decayed, dried out, dried-up, dull, emaciated, withered.

441100 枯槁 kūgǎo: dried, haggard, languid, withered, without energy.

441110 禺 ǒu, yú, yù: abode, accidental, by chance, contain, even-numbers, idol, image, imply, in pairs, legendary monkey of ancient China, live, mate, monkey, noon, pair, reside, residence, spouse.

441200 哉 zāi: alas, final exclamatory or interrogative particle, oh, what a pity, wherefore, why.

441200 神 shēn, shén: amazing, clever, deity, divine essence, energy, God, lively, magical, miraculous, mysterious, power, soul, spirit, spiritual being, supernatural being, unusual, vigour.

441200 神人 shénrén: deity, extraordinary appearance, God, immortal - Taoism, saint.

442100 昏 hūn, mǐn: confused, dark, dusk, faint, lose consciousness, muddle-headed, nightfall, twilight.

442100 昏乱 (昏亂) hūnluàn: chaotic, confused, dazed, decrepit, fuddled, muddleheaded.

442100 昏昏 hūnhūn: very confused.

442100 畏 wēi, wěi, wèi: afraid, awe, dread, fear, flinch, impressive, might, power, recoil in fear, respect, reverence, strength.

442100 畏畏 wèiwèi: extreme fear, fear.

442100 要 yāo, yǎo, yào: ask, coerce, demand, desire, essential, gist, going to - future auxiliary, important, let, main point, may, must, necessary, need, request, serious, should, vital, want, will.

442110 偏 piān: biased, deviation, error, favour, inclined to one side, insist, lean, one-sided, prejudiced, slanting.

442110 损 (損) sǔn: change for the better, damage, decrease, deride, diminish, harm, impair, injure, lose, make fun of, mean, mean - shabby, one of the 64 trigrams of the Book of Changes, reduce, sarcastic, shabby, shrink.

442110 贺 (賀) hè: congratulate, praise, send present.

442200 适 (適) guā, kuò, shì: appropriate, comfortable, control, fast, fit, follow or pursue, go, just now, marry, meet, occasionally, opportune, proper, pursue, quick, rapid, reach, right, suitable, turn towards, well.

442220 棘 jí: brambles, jujube tree, sour jujube, spine, thorn bushes, thorns.

442310 祸 (禍) huò: calamity, disaster, misfortune.

442310 祸福 (禍福) huòfú: disaster and happiness, good and evil, weal and woe.

442311 愚 yú: cheat, deceive, doltish, dull-witted, dupe, fool, foolish, I, ignorant, make fun of, me, silly, stupid.

442311 愚人 yúrén: fool, ignoramus, simpleton, stupid person.

443000 俾 bǐ: cause, enable, in order to, so that.

443020 猛 měng: abruptly, beast of prey, bold, cruel, ferocious, fierce, savage, suddenly, violent.

443020 猛兽 (猛獸) měngshòu: beast of prey, ferocious beast, fierce animal.

443100 缺 quē: deficient, deficit, gap, incomplete, lack, missing, run short of scarce, short of, shortage, vacant post.

443100 缺缺 quēquē: extreme shortage, shortage.

443110 卿 qīng: emperor's form to address minister, high officer, high ranking official, honorific, minister, noble, term of endearment between spouses or friends, term used by the emperor for his subjects.

443110 费 (費) bì, fèi: charge, consume too much, cost, dues, expend too quickly, expenditures, expenses, fee,

nemonik-thinking.org

short-sighted, spend, too many, too much, unable to see clearly, wasteful.

443200 域 yù: area, boundary, district, domain - taxonomy, field, land, realm, region.

443210 蒂 dì: base, base of a flower or fruit, peduncle or stem of plants, stem of fruit.

443400 渢 fēng, féng: buoyant, floating, pleasant sound.

444010 御 (禦) yà, yù: chariot, defend, drive - carriage, drive - chariot, govern, imperial, keep out, manage, resist, ride, ward off.

444200 盗 (盜) dào: bandit, burglar, defraud, escape, illicit intercourse, invade, mobster, pilferer, pirate, plunder, rob, robber, secretly, steal, thief.

444200 盗贼 (盜賊) dàozéi: bandits, criminal, robber, thief.

444300 盜: Mentioned in some versions, but replaced with the simplified 444200 盗.

446010 绵 (綿) mián: continuous, cotton - wad, downy, incessant, mild-mannered, silk floss, silk thread, soft, weak, wool.

446010 绵绵 (綿綿) miánmián: continuous, forever, unbroken, uninterrupted.

nemonik-thinking.org

451100 虽 (雖) suī: also, although, even if, even though.

451100 贵 (貴) guì: admire, cost, costly, dear, expensive, noble, precious, valuable, your name.

451201 患 huàn: contract - disease, danger, disaster, misfortune, suffer - illness, trouble, worry.

451201 患者 huànzhě: patient, sufferer.

452100 罢 (罷) ba, bà, bǎi, pí: abandon idea, cease, dismiss, final particle, finish, forget it, give up, let it be, pass, quit, recall, stop, suspend, terminate.

452100 萧 (蕭) xiāo: bleak, Chinese mugwort, common artemisia, dejected, depressing, desolate, dreary, miserable, mournful, rustle in the air.

452200 凿 (鑿) záo, zuò: authentic, bore a hole, certain, chisel, clear, cut, dig, hole in wood, irrefutable, pierce chisel, true.

453110 常 cháng: always, common, constant, ever, frequent, general, invariable, normal, norms, often, ordinary, regular, universal, usually.

453110 常有 chángyǒu: more often than not, often, usually.

454201 德 dé: character, ethics, favour, goodness, heart, kind, kindness, mind, moral character, moral excellence, morality, morals, virtue.

455210 纍 luó: basket, basket for carrying earth.

455300 褒 bāo: cite, commend, extol, honour, large or loose clothes, praise, speak favourably.

456100 微 wēi: abstruse, decline, insubstantial, micro, micron, miniature, minute, one millionth, prefix micro-, profound, slightly, small, tiny, trifling.

456100 微妙 wēimiào: delicate, subtle, subtlety, wonderful.

456100 微明 wēimíng: dim or faint light, twilight.

456100 微眇 wēimiǎo, wēimiào: small, trifling, very slight.

456100 微细 wēixì: micro, small, very small.

461000 屈 qū: bend, bent, bow, crooked, crouch, feel wronged, flex, inconvenience, injustice, subdue, submit, wrong, yield.

462020 揣 chuāi, chuǎi, chuài, tuán, zhuī: carry in one's clothes, conceal, cram, estimate, figure, guess, hammer, hide or carry in one's clothes, holding, impose one's views etc. on others, measure, overeat, overfeed,

nemonik-thinking.org

pregnant, put into, put things under clothes, ram, strike, struggle, surmise.

462100 葆 bǎo: conceal, cover, defend, dense foliage, keep, nurture, preserve, protect, reserve, retain.

462210 湍 tuān, zhuān: clean, rapid, rapid water current, rapids, rush, rushing water, scour, swift, torrential, turbulent.

470000 盅 chōng, zhōng: cup, cup without handle, empty, goblet, handleless cup, hollow, small cup or bowl, void.

500000

503210 朕 zhèn: chink, eyeballs, foretaste, I, I - used by emperor or king, my, omen, portent, pronoun - I, sign, subtle, warn, we - imperial use.

503410 海 hǎi: extra-large, lake, maritime, ocean, sea.

504210 笃 (篤) dǔ: concentrate, critical, deep, devoted, faithful, genuine, reliable, serious - illness, sincere, true, trustful, very ill.

506510 察 chá: check, clearly evident, examine, inquire, inspect, investigate, look into, look over, notice, observe, obvious, scrutinize, see, strict.

506510 察察 cháchá: astute, clean, examining, scrutinize, sharp eye, spotless, very strict.

511100 奉 fèng: accept orders, attend, believe - religion, esteem, fawn upon, flatter, give, offer tribute, present respectfully, receive, receive from superior, respect, revere, serve, wait upon.

512110 契 qì, qiè, xiè: agree, agreement, bond, carved words - engraved, contract, deed, engrave.

512120 服 bì, fú, fù: acclimatize, accustomed, adapt, clothes, comply, convince, dose - medicine, dress, garment, medicine, mourning clothes, obey, serve, submit, take, take medicine, wear, wear mourning clothes.

512210 梼 (檮) dǎo, táo: block of wood, blockhead, bonehead, dunce, pestle, pound to pieces, pound with a pestle, smash, stupid.

514200 浑 (渾) gǔn, hún, hùn: all, all over, at all, billow, blend, confused, drift recklessly, foolish, honest, merge, mix, muddled, muddy, natural, pure, roll, simple, still, stupid, surge, surging sound, theory that the Earth is inside heaven, torrent, turbid, unsophisticated, vast, whole, yet.

514200 浑浑 (渾渾) húnhún: merge extremely.

515410 媮 tōu, yú: handsome.

520100 言 yán, yàn, yín: Chinese character, declaration, say, saying, speak, speech, talk, word.

520100 言者 yánzhě: speaker.

521020 捕 bǔ: arrest, capture, catch, seize.

521101 起 qǐ: appear, batch, begin, case, draft, establish, events, extract, get from a depot or counter, get up, go up, groups, grow, initiate action, instance, launch, pull, raise, rise, set out, stand up, start, starting from - place or time, up, verb suffix.

521110 享 xiǎng: benefit, enjoy, have the use of.

521200 洼 (窪) guī, wā: depression, hollow place, low, pit, sunken, swamp, winding ditch.

521200 音 yīn, yìn: news, noise, note on musical scale, pitch, pronunciation, reading - phonetic value of a character, sound, syllable, tidings, tone.

522000 吾 wú: I, impede, me, my, our, resist, we.

522100 宜 yí: appropriate, better, fit, fitting, of course, ought, proper, right, should, suitable, would be better.

522100 首 shǒu: chief, first, head, leader, poems, songs.

522110 亭 tíng: booth, erect, kiosk, pavilion, straight up, suitable average.

522110 推 tuī: choice, clip, cut, decline, deduce, delay, elect, expel, further, give impetus to, infer, nominate, planet, postpone, push, push forward, put off, refuse, refuse responsibility, reject, shirk responsibility, shove.

522200 难 (難) nán, nàn, nuó: arduous, bad, difficult, disaster, distress, hard, hardly possible, not good, problem, put somebody in difficult position, scold, unable, unpleasant.

522200 难得 (難得) nándé: hard to come by, rare, seldom.

522200 难易 (難易) nányì: degree of difficulty or ease, difficult.

522200 难治 (难難) nánzhì: difficult to cure.

522211 尊 zūn: cannon, esteem, honorific, honour, respect, revere, senior, senior generation, statues, venerate, wine vessel, your.

522310 焉 yān, yí: how, so that, then, therefore, thereupon, where, why.

522320 渝 yú: alter, change.

522401 意 yì: anticipate, desire, expect, idea, intention, meaning, opinion, think, thought, wish.

523100 复 (復, 複) fù: again, answer, carry out, cave, complex - not simple, composite, compound, cover,

nemonik-thinking.org

diplo-, double, dress, duplicated, every time, go and return, lined garment, overlap, protect, recover, remit, repair, repeat, reply - letter, reproduce, restore, resume, retaliate, return, revenge, shelter, turn around, turn back, turn over, turn reply.

523100 复命 (復命) fùmìng: debriefing, report on completion of a task.

523100 复归 (復歸) fùguī: come back, return, revert.

523100 轻 (輕) qīng: belittle, disparage, easy, frivolous, gentle, light - weight, low voice, neutral, rash, reckless, relaxed, simple, slight, small in number or degree, soft, unimportant, unstressed.

523100 轻敌 (輕敵) qīngdí: belittle the enemy, take the enemy lightly, underestimate the enemy.

523101 既 jì, xì: already, as, as well as, both and, de facto, now that, since, since, then.

523101 既得 jìdé: already obtained, vested - e.g. interest.

523101 既有 jìyǒu: both, existing, if I had known it would come to this then I would have acted differently, if it has to be like this now then it's a pity it was even like that in the beginning, if there must be today then why should there have been other days.

523110 琭 lù: jade, jade like stone.

523110 琭琭 lùlù: great splendour, rare, scarce.

523110 诤 (諍) zhēng, zhèng: admonish, criticize frankly, expostulate, frank advice, frankly, rebuke, remonstrate, warn somebody of their errors.

523111 脱 (脫) tuō: come off, divorced, escape, get away, leave, left out, omitted, separated, shed, shedding of hair, take off.

523200 冥 míng: absorbed, abstruse, close, confused, dark, deep, die out, dimly, dull, excellent, far-reaching, gloomy, Gods, hollow, ignorant, muddle-headed, nature, nether world, night, obscure, ocean, profound and lasting, quiet, sea, silent, stupid, stupid, tacit agreement, underworld, void, wonderful.

523210 寄 jì: consign, depend, entrust, hopes, live in a house, lodge, mail, post, rely on, send, transmit.

523300 逢 féng, páng, péng: come across, come upon, every time, fawn upon, flatter, happen meet, meet by chance.

523301 猷 yóu: grand plan, plan, plot, scheme, way.

nemonik-thinking.org

523320 翕 xī, xì: agree, amiable, close, concentrate, deflate, fold, furl, harmonious, shut amiable and compliant.

524100 敢 gǎn: bold, brave, courageous, daring, venture.

524100 敢为 gǎnwéi: act with courage and determination, dare to do.

524200 宴 (讌) yàn: banquet, dinner, entertain, feast, host a dinner, relax, repose, spread.

524200 锉 (剉, 銼) cuò: carpenter's file, file - tool, file smooth, filing, smooth – file.

524200 雄 xióng: grand, hero, heroic, imposing, male, manly, mighty, person or state having great power and influence, powerful, stamina.

524210 敦 diāo, duī, duì, dūn, tuán, tún: administer, advise, attach great importance - weight to, attach great weight to, bring under control, candid, cordial, cordial, courage, diligent, eating vessel, encourage, esteem, govern, grain receptacle, harness, honest, intimate, kind-hearted, manage, put in order, rich, run, sincere, stocky, thick, urge.

524211 隐 (隱) yǐn, yìn: conceal, crypto-, Greek stem, hidden, hide, lean upon, secret.

524300 登 dé, dēng: ascend, board, climb, enter e.g. in a register, gathered and taken to the threshing ground, go up, issue, mount, note, press down with foot, publish or record, record, register, rise, scale a height, step on, step or tread on, tread.

524410 蔡 cài: big tortoise, big turtle, species of tortoise, turtle, wild grass.

526210 豪 háo: bold, brave, bullying, chivalrous, despotic, forthright, giant, grand, heroic, outstanding, person of extraordinary powers, power, powerful, unconstrained, unrestrained.

528220 豫 yù, xù: at ease, beforehand, big elephant, carefree, comfortable, happy, pleased, prefecture, prepare, relaxed.

530000 里 (裏, 裡) lǐ: administrative unit, here, home, hometown, inner, inside, interior, internal, lane, lining - clothing, neighbour, neighbourhood, unit of length - 500 meters, village, within.

530100 国 (國) guó: Chinese, country, nation, national, state, of our country, Universe, unlimited space, without name, capital, country, emperor's, feud, hometown, national, nation-state, place, state, tribe.

nemonik-thinking.org

530100 国中 guózhōng: junior.

530100 国家 (國家) guójiā: country, households governed by a nation, nation, state.

531000 君 jūn: gentleman, lord, monarch, ruler, sovereign, supreme ruler, you.

531000 君子 jūnzǐ: gentleman, great man, man of noble character, nobleman, person of higher class or position, person with high morality, person with high position.

531000 者 zhě, zhū: after a noun - person involved in, after a verb or adjective, elder, -er - person, false, former, frivolous, he who, indicates a thing, -ist, it, latter, mark a pause before defining the term, one who, person who does something, pretext, refer to something mentioned previously, suffix: -ist or -er or -ing, that, that which, them, they, thing, this, those, those who, used after a term, used at the end of a command, who.

531010 周 (週, 賙) zhōu: all, all over, attentive, bestow alms, circle, circuit, circumference, complete, cycle, encircle, every, help financially, lap, make a circuit, thorough, thoughtful, week, weekly, widespread.

531010 甹 pīng, píng: chivalrous knight, gallant man.

531100 信 shēn, xìn: at random, at will, believe, confidence, evidence, faith, information, letter, mail, profess faith in, proof, religious, sign, sincere, true, trust, truth, truthful.

531100 恒 (恆) héng: always, common, constant, eternal, fixed, forever, keep long time, lasting, often, one of the 64 trigrams, ordinary, permanent, perseverance, persistent, regular, rule, usual.

531100 恒心 (恆心) héngxīn: perseverance.

531100 昧 mèi: against, conceal, dark, dim-sighted, fatuous, hazy, ignorant, muddle-headed, obscure, poor-vision, stupid.

531100 是 (乃) shì: all, am, any, are, be, correct, demonstrative pronoun, important affair, indeed, is, it, justify, praise, right, sure, that, these, this, true, yes.

531100 是以 shìyǐ: so, so that, that is why, then, therefore, thus.

531100 是故 shìgù: consequently, so, that is why, therefore.

531100 甚: Mentioned in some versions, but replaced with the simplified 121000 什.

nemonik-thinking.org

531100 相 xiāng, xiàng: alike, appearance, assist, each other, evaluate, judge, minister, mutual, one another, picture, portrait, reciprocal, similar.

531100 相加 xiāngjiā: add together, adding, addition.

531100 相去 xiāngqù, xiàngqù: apart, apart from one another, at a distance.

531100 相合 xiānghé: agree with, compatible, conform, fit.

531100 相形 xiāngxíng: by comparison, by contrast.

531100 相望 xiāngwàng: face each other, look at each other, one official is succeeded by another, sea.

531100 相生 xiāngshēng: engender one another, interpromoting relation in five elements.

531100 相若 xiāngruò: about the same, alike, comparable to, on a par with, similar.

531100 相较 (相較) xiāngjiào: compare.

531100 隼 sǔn, zhǔn: aquiline nose, Falco peregrinus, falcon, peregrine falcon.

531120 呜 (鳴) míng: chirp, cry of bird or animal, express, make sound, sound, voice.

nemonik-thinking.org

531200 洁 (潔) jí, jié: Buddhist monk, clean, clear distinction, concise, distinguish, honest, keep clean, preserve purity, pure, purify, spotless, white

532000 鱼 (魚) yú: fish.

532100 官 guān: government, government cadre, government official, government owned, military official, officeholder, officer, official, organ of body, public servant.

532110 勇 yǒng: brave, courageous, fierce, valiant.

532110 勇于 (勇於) yǒngyú: brave enough to, dare, have the courage to.

532110 得 de, dé, děi: accumulate, achieve, acquire, allow, can, catch - disease, caught, complacent, contented, degree or possibility, equal, finished, fit, gain, get, have to, linking it to following phrase indicating effect, may, must, need, obtain, ought to, particle used after a verb show effect, permit, possibility, proper, proud, ready, receive, result, satisfied, seize, suitable, sure, take.

532110 得力 délì: able, capable, competent, efficient.

532110 得名 démíng: get one's name, named, named after something.

nemonik-thinking.org

532110 得志 (得誌) dézhì: accomplish one's ambition, achieve one's ambition, dream come true, success, successful career.

532110 捨: Mentioned in some versions, but replaced with the simplified 431100 舍.

532200 培 péi, pǒu: bank up with dirt, breed, bring up, cultivate, earth up, foster, grow, train.

532200 惧 (懼) jù: afraid, dread, fear, scare.

532200 眯 (瞇) mī, mí, mǐ, mì: blind - with dust, blinded, get into eye, squint, take a nap.

532200 谁 (誰) shéi, shuí: anyone, everyone, someone, who, whom, whose.

532210 陪 péi: accompany, assist, be with, go with, keep company, look after, serve, show.

532300 進: Mentioned in some versions, but replaced with the simplified 322200 进.

532320 逾 dòu, yú: cross over, exceed, go beyond, go over, jump over, pass over, transcend.

533100 斯 sī: emphatic particle, here, lop off, such, that is, the, then, therefore, this, thus.

533100 破 pò: break, broken, capture a city, cleave, cut, damaged, defeat, destroy, expose the truth, get rid of, lousy, rout, ruin, spend, split, worn out.

533120 郭店 Guōdiàn: Guodian version of Lao Zi's Dao De Jing.

533200 尟 xiǎn: few, fresh, rare.

533201 混 gǔn, hún, hǔn, hùn, kūn: aimlessly, all, band, bind, blend, bumble along, careless, confused, cord, dirty, drift along, fool, get along with somebody, irresponsible, lurk, make trouble, merge, mingle, mix, muddle along, muddled, muddy, palm off as, pass for, pass off as, reckless, string, tape, thoughtless, torrent, trim, turbid, unite, whole.

533300 廉 lián: angle, break, cheap, clean, clear, corner, edge, hold two or more jobs concurrently, honest, honest and clean man, honest and upright, honourable, incorrupt, inexpensive, inspect, integrity, investigate, low-priced, narrow, sharp, side - hall - house, tiny, upright.

533310 孰 shú: what, which, who.

533310 暴 bào, pù, bó: brutal, bulge, cruel, expose, injure, ruin, show, sudden, tyrannical, vicious, violent.

nemonik-thinking.org

533310 暴雨 bàoyǔ: downpour, gush, hard rain, intense fall, rainstorm, squall, torrential rain.

533500 默 mò: dark, quiet, silent, still.

534100 埏 shān, yán: boundary, clay, mix water with clay, outlying place, path to grave, tomb passage.

534101 锐 (鋭, 銳) duì, ruì, yuè: abrupt, acute, angle, drastic, drive, keen, motivation, pointed, sharp, vigour.

534202 稽 jī, qǐ: bow to the ground, calculate, check, concerned, consult, delay, examine, find fault, inquire, inspect, investigate, procrastinate, stop, take to heart.

534300 赛 (賽) sài: better than, competition, contend, contest, excel, match, outdo, race, superior, surpass.

534310 勢: Mentioned in some versions, but replaced with the simplified 313220 势.

534610 熟 shóu, shú: cooked - food, done, familiar, mature - seeds, ripe - fruit, skilled, well-cooked.

535100 復: Mentioned in some versions, but replaced with the simple 523100 复.

536520 彌: Mentioned in some versions, but replaced with the simplified 414120 弥.

540000 昔 cuò, xī, xí: ancient, begin, former, former days, former times, formerly, past, past time.

540010 呵 (啊, 诃) a, ā, á, ǎ, à, hā, hē, kē: abuse, bend one's back, berate, bow, breathe out with the mouth open, cater, confirmation, cradle of Chinese nation, drink, exclamation, exclamatory particle, exhale, expel breath, expressing surprise, expression of recognition - oh it's you, happy, hay, hoot, interjection of agreement- uhm - ah - OK, interjection of doubt or question - show realization - to stress- eh - what, interjection of surprise - ah - oh - eh - my - what's up, laugh, modal particle ending sentence - affirmation - approval - consent, my goodness, o, obey or yield reluctantly, oh, oho, on and on, pander, phonetic particle, really, rebuke, scold, stoop, yawn, yell, yes.

541000 居 jī, jū: appoint, assert, bedrooms, certain position, claim, dwell, final particle expressing doubt, harbouring, house, lay by, live, occupy, reside, residence, restaurant, standstill, stay, store up, style oneself.

541000 居前 (居前) jīqián, jūqián: in front.

541010 吼 hōu, hǒu, xū: bellow, breathe, howl, roar, yawn.

nemonik-thinking.org

541100 悝 huī, kuī, lǐ: afflicted, laugh, ridicule, rustic, sad, unrefined, vulgar, worried.

541100 莫 mò, mù: cannot, do not, is not, negative, nobody, not, nothing, there is none who.

541100 莫不 mòbù: everyone, none doesn't, there is no one who does not or is not ... e.g. inspired, there is none who isn't.

541100 莫大 mòdà: greatest, most important.

541100 莫能 mònéng: love but have no ability to help, there is no exception to this rule, unable to help even for the sake of love, willing to help but unable to do so.

541100 莫若 mòruò: might as well, would be better.

541100 诘 (詰) jié: ask for explanation if mistake is made, examined, inquire, interrogate, investigate, question, restrain, scold.

541210 傅奕 Fu Yi: Chinese philosopher Fu Yi (555 – 639 AD), version of Lao Zi's Dao De Jing.

542010 猎 (獵) liè, què, xí: field sports, hunting.

542100 珸 wú: double-edged sword, gem, jade-like stone – gem.

542200 普 pǔ: everywhere, general, popular, universal, widespread.

542200 谋 (謀) móu: cleverness, consult, device, plan, plot, scheme, seek, stratagem, work for.

542300 貸: Mentioned in some versions, but replaced with the simplified 143300 贷.

542310 通 tōng, tòng: clear, clear out, coherent, common, communicate, connect, go through, inform, know well, letters, music, normally, open, pass through, phone calls, telegrams, through, understand, unpleasant language, workable.

543100 堂 táng: auditorium, classes, classroom, government office, hall, large room, main hall, relationship between cousins on paternal side, room, same clan, sets of furniture.

543100 順: Mentioned in some versions, but replaced with the simplified 243100 顺.

543110 盈 yíng: fill, fill to the brim, filled, full, imbued, overflowing, superfluous, surplus.

543300 落落 làlà, làolào, luōluō, luòluò: aloof, dignified, graceful, natural, pile up, poised, standoffish, unsociable.

544210 播 bō, bǒ, bò: broadcast, case away, exile move about, reject, scatter, seed, sow, spread.

nemonik-thinking.org

545001 绳 (繩) mǐn, shéng, yìng: control, cord, rope, string.

545001 绳绳 (繩繩) mǐnmǐn, shéngshéng, yìngyìng: cautious, continuous, infinite, trance, unending.

545200 稷 jì, zè: god of cereals, god of grains, millet, minister of agriculture.

545300 辎 (輜) zī: covered wagon, dray, military supply, supply cart, wagon.

545310 螫 shì, zhē: bite, poison, poisonous insect, sting.

550000 固 gù: admittedly, as a matter of course, assuredly, become solid, certainly, chronic, consolidate, determined, firm, hard, in the first place, indeed, inveterate, of course, original, resolute, solid, solidify, strengthen, strong, sure, undoubtedly.

550000 草 cǎo, zào: careless, draft of a document, grass, hasty, herbs, illegible, manuscript, rough, straw, thatch.

550000 草木 cǎomù: grass and trees, plants, vegetation.

550000 革 gé, jí, jǐ: animal hide, change, expel, leather, reform, remove.

551100 盖 (蓋) gài, gě, hé: block out, build, canopy, cover, cover up, hide, lid, protect, shell, stamp, top.

nemonik-thinking.org

551100 诺 (諾) nuò: approve, assent, consent, promise, yes.

552100 跂 jī, qí, qǐ, qì: base, climb, crawling, creeping, extra toe, foot, foot with six toes, foundation, get rid of, hope for, jump, lean against, lean on, long for, look forward to, peak, resist, sit with feet hanging, sit with legs hanging, sixth extra toe, stand on tiptoe, top.

552120 隅 yú: brink, corner, edge, nook, remote place, verge.

552300 溃 (潰) kuì: break down, break through an encirclement, burst - dike or dam, collapse, decompose, defeat, dispersed, fester, flooding river, militarily defeat, obtain, overflow, reach, routed, ulcerate, utterly defeated.

552310 遇 yù: chance, come across, encounter, meet, opportunity, receive, treat, treatment.

553110 属 (屬) shǔ, zhǔ: affiliated, belong, born in the year of one of the 12 animals, category, class, concentrate, constitute, dependents, family members, fix one's attention, focus, genus - taxonomy, join together, prove, subordinate, to be, type, under.

nemonik-thinking.org

553300 潇 (瀟) xiāo: deep and clear – water, sound of rain and wind.

553301 燕 yān, yàn: bird's nest, carefree, close, comfort, easy, enjoy, entertain - dinner, intimate, peaceful, profane, quiet, relaxed, slight, swallow - bird, tailcoat, white-neck duck.

557910 臘: Mentioned in some versions, but replaced with the simplified 841010 腊.

562110 阖 (闔) gé, hé: all, close, council-chamber, door, entire, leaf, shelf, shut, side door, whole.

562200 嗌 ài, yì: choke, quarrel, throat, throat.

562200 淈 gǔ: blend, confuse, disorder, drain, dry up, exhaust, mess, mingle, mix, muddle, muddy, murky world.

562200 遗 (遺) wèi, yí: bequeath, heritage, inheritance, involuntary discharge - urine etc., keep, leave behind, leave out, legacy, lose, loss, lost, miss, omit, remain, stay, suitable, unfulfilled.

600000

603310 筹 (籌) chóu: arrow, chip - gambling, counter, devise, manage, map out, means, plan, plot, prepare,

nemonik-thinking.org

raise money, resource, scheme, tally, ticket, token for counting.

603310 筹策 chóucè: bamboo sticks, moves, plan, policy, procedures, strategy.

604021 脆 cuì: brittle, clear, crisp, crunchy, enunciated, fragile, frail, loud voice, neat.

604220 勝: Mentioned in some versions, but replaced with the simplified 612010 胜.

604220 筋 jīn, qián: muscle, rubber band, tendon, vein.

611210 毒 dài, dú: ancient - mature, calamity, crime, cruel, drug, evil, fierce, hate, heavy, hot, injure, kill with poison, malevolent, malicious, manage, narcotics, noxious, pain, poison, severe, suffering, thick, toxin, venom, vicious, violent.

612010 胜 (勝) shēng, shèng: able, beat, beautiful scenery, better than, competent, defeat someone else, equal to task, excel, get the better of, overcome, overcome, peptide, success, superb of vista, superior, surpass, triumph, victory, win, wonderful view.

615400 辨 bān, bàn, biǎn, biàn, piàn: discriminate, distinguish, distinguish, recognize.

616400 辍 (輟) chuò: cease, halt, stop, suspend.

nemonik-thinking.org

620000 非 fēi, fěi: blame, illegal, in-, incorrect, insist, negative, non-, not, oppose, reproach, run counter to, simply must, un-, wrong.

620000 非可 fēikě, fēikè: nonerasable, storage.

620000 非常 fēicháng: exceptional, extraordinary, extreme, unusual, very.

620000 非正统 fēizhèngtǒng: unorthodox.

621000 直 zhí: directly, erect, fair, frank, indicates continuing motion or action), keep on, reasonable, straight, straighten, straightforward, upright, vertical.

621000 直觉 zhíjué: intuition.

621010 明 míng: able, bright, brilliant, clear, clear of meaning, clear-sighted, clever, distinct, enlighten, Farmer God, fourth of the legendary Flame Emperors, generic term for a sacrifice to the gods, intelligent, light, look, next, openly, opposite of dark, overt, perceptive, public or open, sharp-eyed, show, sight, understand, watch, wise.

621010 明白 míngbai: clear, know, obvious, realize, understand, unequivocal.

621100 春 chūn, chǔn: gay, joyful, life, love, lust, spring, vitality, wanton, youthful.

nemonik-thinking.org

621201 悲 bēi: compassion, sad, grief, sad, sadness, sorrow, sorry.

621201 悲哀 bēi'āi: grief, grievous, look blue, mourn, pathetic, sad, sorrow, woe.

621201 悲泣 bēiqì: sob, wail, weep with grief.

622010 厚 hòu: deep, depth, favour, generous, greatly, kind, large, magnanimous, profound, rich or strong in flavour, stress, substantial, thick, thick for flat things.

622100 真 zhēn: actual, authentic, clear, distinct, factual, genuine, indeed, real, really, true, truly, unmistakably.

622301 蠢 chǔn: blunt, fat, silly, stupid, wiggle – worms.

622301 蠢蠢 chǔnchǔn: very stupid.

622310 淳 chún, zhūn, zhǔn: genuine, honest, pure, simple, unsophisticated.

622310 淳淳 chúnchún: very pure, very simple.

622400 誉 (譽) yù: eulogize, fame, honorary, praise, reputation.

623110 握 wò: grasp, grip, hold fast, master, shake hands, take by hand.

623200 短 duǎn: brief, deficient, fault, lack, run short of, short, weak point.

623210 摄 (攝) niè, shè: absorb, act, act as deputy, assimilate, assist, collect, conserve one's health, keep, photo, take in.

624220 弱 ruò: delicate, feeble, fragile, inferior, weak, young.

625500 澄 chéng, dèng: clarify, clear, clear sky, limpid, make clear, pure, purify, purify water by allowing sediment to settle, settle liquid.

626420 歙 shè, xī: clutch, fold, furl, grasp, hold, inhale, shut, suck.

626420 歙 歙 shèshè, xīxī: carefully, restrain.

630010 事 shì: accident, affair, approach, business, doing, effort, engage, event, incident matter, involvement, item, job, matter, responsibility, serve, thing, trouble, wait upon, work.

630100 盲 máng: blind, short-sighted, unperceptive.

631000 垣 yuán: city wall, low wall, town, wall.

631000 重 chóng, tóng, zhòng: again, attach importance, considerable, deep, discreet, double, duplicate, heavy, important, iterate, layer, momentous, more than usual size, once more, pay great attention, place value on, prudent, put stress on, repeat, serious, severely, weight.

631002 配 pèi: accompany, allocate, blend, compound, deserve, equal, fit, have a key made, join, make up - a prescription, marry, match, mate, mix, pair, replace, spouse, suit.

631100 基 jī: base, basic, essential, foundation, fundamental, radical - chemistry, rudimentary.

631110 情 qíng: affection, circumstances, condition, emotion, favour, feeling, kindness, love, passion, sensibility, sentiment, situation, state of affairs.

631200 章 zhāng, zhàng: article, badge, become visible, big timber, button, chapter, clauses, coloured silks, commend, commendation, composition, decorative pattern, decrees, figure, flag, inform against, institutions, medal, movement - of symphony, order, orderliness, paragraph, praise, proper presentation, regulation, remarkable, rules, seal, section, song, sub-clauses, systematic, tree, written report to the emperor.

631220 搏 bó: beat, combat, fight, pounce on, pulsate, seize, spring upon, strike, struggle, throb, wrestle.

nemonik-thinking.org

632100 惷 chǔn: delighted, happy, pleased, wriggle.

632100 惷惷 chǔnchǔn: very happy.

632100 奢 shē: exaggerate, extravagance, luxurious, wasteful.

632100 害 hài, hé: bane, calamity, cause trouble, contract a disease, danger, destroy, disaster, evil, harm, injure, kill, murder, pest, unjustly kill.

632110 散 sǎn, sàn: adjourn, break up, break up of couples, come apart, come loose, disband, disperse, distribute, fire or discharge somebody, leisurely, let out, loose, loosen, powdered medicine, scatter.

632110 超 chāo, chǎo, chào, tiào: cross, exceed, jump over, leap over, overtake, pass, super, surpass, transcend, ultra-.

632110 超然 chāorán: aloof, detached, distracted, stand aloof.

632110 辅 (輔) fǔ: assist, auxiliary, cheek bone, complement, complement, protective.

632200 善 shàn: apt, benevolent, charitable, competent, expert, familiar, friendly, good, good at something, honest, improve or perfect, kind, kind good, know how, liable, perfect, proper, satisfaction, skilled, success, virtuous, well, well-disposed, wise.

632200 善人 shànrén: charitable person, philanthropist, well-doer.

632200 善用 shànyòng: good at using something, use.

632200 善能 shànnéng: be good at.

632200 善行 shànxíng: good actions, good conduct, kind deed.

632200 善言 shànyán: good words, kind words.

632300 湛 chén, dān, jiān, jìn, tán, zhàn: approach perfection, clear, clear as water, consummate, crystal, crystal clear, dark blue, deep, dewy, full, invisible, lucid, placid, profound, tranquil, transparent.

633120 输 (輸) shū: carry, donate, enter a password, haul, lose, transport.

633200 塞 sāi, sài, sè: block, cope, cork, cram, fortress, frontier, pack, pass, piston, seal, squeeze in, stop up, stopper, strategic pass, stuff, tactical border position, unenlightened.

633210 極: Mentioned in some versions, but replaced with the simplified 314200 极.

633210 碌 liù, lù, luò: busy, common place, employ, hire, laborious, malachite, mediocre, quivering, record, rocky, rough, shaking, small stone, tape, uneven, write down.

633210 碌碌 lùlù: busy with miscellaneous work, common place, laborious, mediocre, ordinary, toilsome.

633220 随 (隨) suí: accompany, according, adapt, allow, along with other action, carry on, comply with, follow, go with, let somebody do as he likes, listen to, look like, one of the 64 divinatory Symbols, please oneself, resemble, submit, varying according to.

633300 道 dǎo, dào: dao, daoism, direction, discuss, line, long thin stretches, method, morality, path, principle, reason, rivers, road, say, skill, speak, street, talk, tao of taoism, the Way, truth, way.

633300 道德经 (道德經) Dàodéjīng: book by Lao Zi, sacred text of Daoism, Way Virtue Classic – literally.

633310 渴 hé, jié, kài, kě: drain, eager, imperative, parched, pine, pressing, thirsty, urgent, watery, yearn.

634200 彰 zhāng: clear, evident, manifest, obvious, praise.

634200 握 wò: grasp, master, wooden screen.

nemonik-thinking.org

634200 窘 jiǒng: awkward position, deliberately try to embarrass somebody, dilemma, distressed, embarrassed, exhausted, hard-pressed, impoverished.

634210 歇 xiē, yà: cease, have a rest, lodge, rest, stop.

634210 赘 (贅) zhuì: cumbersome, hindrance, redundant, slowing down, son-in-law living with wife's family, superfluous, unnecessary, useless.

634310 竭 jié: drain, dry up, exhaust, great effort, use up.

636210 徼 jiāo, jiǎo, jiào, yāo, yáo: border, boundary, expose, frontier, go around, hide, inspect, inspection tour, limit, mere luck, path, patrol, pray, steal, tangle.

639210 骤 (驟) zhòu, zòu: abrupt, gallop, procedure, sudden, unexpected.

639210 骤雨 (驟雨) zhòuyǔ: brash, heavy shower, shower, sudden downpour.

639510 纇 lèi: blemish, entangled silken knots, flaw, hold those, knot, wicked.

640210 博 bó: abundant, aim, ample, big, broad, broad extensive, erudite, extensive, gain, gamble, get, knowledgeable, large, learned, obtain, play games, plentiful, possess wide knowledge, profound, rich, well-read, wide, wide knowledge, win.

nemonik-thinking.org

641010 措 cuò: administer, arrange, collect, employ, execute, handle, make plans, manage, place, plan, put in order, strike, take action.

641010 昭 zhāo: bright, clear, distinct, evident, illustrious, luminous, manifest, obvious, show clearly.

641010 昭昭 zhāozhāo: bright, clear, light, obvious, plain, understand, very clear, visible, well-lit, worry.

641100 唯 wéi, wěi: agreement, alone, but, except that, flatter, have no will of one's own, -ism, obsequious, only, whatever you say, yes, yes-man.

641100 唯有 wéiyǒu: only.

642010 据 (據) jū, jù: according to, act in accordance, base, depend, evidence, foundation, occupy, position, rely on, seize, sickness of hand, take possession.

642010 据鸟 jùniǎo: bird of prey.

642010 骨 gū, gú, gǔ: back bone, bone, character trait, frame, framework, moral integrity, quality, skeleton.

642100 楮 chǔ, zhū: book, mulberry, paper, paper money, paper mulberry.

642100 语 (語) yǔ, yù: dialect, expression, language, saying, speak, speech, tell, words.

642100 诸 (諸) zhū: all, at, every, from, many, these, to, various.

642110 割 gē: cede, cut, cut apart, cut off, divide, partition.

642200 慎 shèn: act with care, careful, cautious.

642200 辞 (辭) cí: bid farewell, decline, diction, discharge, dismiss, evade, expression, literature, phrase, phraseology, poetry, refined language, resign, say goodbye, shirk, speech, take leave, wording, words.

642310 漂 biāo, piāo, piǎo, piào: bleach, drift, elegant, fail float, polished, rinse, tossed about

643000 铦 (銛) xiān: arm implements, fish, fish fork, hoe, keen-edged, sharp, sharp knife, sharp weapon, spade, spear.

643001 晚 wǎn: evening, late, night, not on time.

643100 硌 gè: big stone on mountain, bulging, cause pain through pressure, hard, large stone, pressing, rock, rub, stack up.

643100 硌硌 gègè: cackle, chuckle, cluck, presses, titter.

643200 寞 mò: lonely, lonesome, quiet, silent, solitary, still.

643200 蜂 fēng: bee, hornet, wasp.

nemonik-thinking.org

643310 噤 jìn: close, keep silent, shiver, silent, unable to speak.

644100 傾: Mentioned in some versions, but replaced with the simplified 344100 倾.

644310 褐 hé, hè: brown, cheap cloth, coarse cloth or clothing, coarse cotton garments, coarse hemp cloth, coarse woollen cloth, dark colour, dull, grey, hempen socks.

645100 馆 (館) guǎn: accommodation for guests, building, embassy or consulate, establishment, guest house, hall, hotel, house, live, museum, public building, reside, schoolroom, shop, stay, term for certain service establishments.

645101 魄 bó, pò, tuò: body, bold, casual, courage, dark, dark part of moon, dire straits, distiller's grains, distraction, down-and-out, energy, flimsy, lose one's soul - wits, morning or evening moonlight, part of moon, resolution, soul, sound of falling on ground, spirit, thin, unconventional, untrammelled by convention, vigour.

nemonik-thinking.org

650110 高 gāo, gào: above average, above normal, advanced, brilliant, elevated, height, high, lofty, loud, superior, tall, your.

650110 高下 gāoxià: relative superiority - better or worse - stronger or weaker - above or below, superiority and inferiority.

651100 兽 (獸) shòu: animal, beast, beastly, bestial, quadruped.

651100 啬 (嗇) sè: frugal, miserly, stingy, thrifty.

651110 畸 jī, qí: abnormal, fractional, irregular, lopsided, odd, odd fractional remnant, odd lots, remainder, unbalanced.

652310 谪 (謫) zhé: banish, blame, censure, charge, demote, disgrace, exile, expel, find fault, relegate.

653100 雌 cī, cí: female, feminine, gentle, soft.

653101 塵: Mentioned in some versions, but replaced with the simplified 221100 尘.

653310 飘 (飄) piāo: at ease, blow, cyclone, drift about, fail, fall, flare, float, flutter, fly in the air, free from affectation, graceful, profound, rapid, remote, smug, storm wind, strong wind, swift, to and fro, wander, whirlwind, wobble.

653310 飘风 (飄) piāofēng: cyclone, stormy wind, violent storm, violent wind, whirlwind.

653410 爵 jué: ancient bronze wine holder with 3 legs and loop handle, beaker, feudal title or rank, give position of nobility, nobility.

661100 曼 mán, màn: beautiful, extended, graceful, handsome, large, long, prolonged, vast.

661301 熙 xī: bright, bustling, exposed to the sun, gay, glorious, happy, merry, play, prosperous, rise, splendid, sunny.

661301 熙熙 xīxī: bustling, comfort, ease, large crowd, merry, very happy.

662000 营 (營) yíng: abide in fortified village, army, barracks, battalion, build, camp, construct, deal in, encamp, handle, headquarters, manage, measure, nourishment, operate, provide, pursue, puzzle, run, running of business, seek, trade, wind around.

662000 营魄 (營魄) yíngpò: battalion spirit, camp soul, corps de esprit, team spirit.

673001 兢 jīng: cautious, fearful, move, strong, apprehensive, careful, cautious, fearful, strong, twitch, wary.

700000

721210 清 qīng, qìng: check-up, clarified, clean, clean up, clear, clear up, cold, complete, count, distinct, just and honest, nothing left, peaceful, pure, purge, quiet, settle, simple, take inventory, thoroughly, unmixed.

721210 清静 (清靜) qīngjìng: peaceful, quiet.

722100 建 jiàn: advocate, build, construct, erect, establish, found, propose, put up, set up, build, construct, erect, establish, found, set up.

722100 建言 jiànyán: declare, offer advice or suggestions, state, state one's views and proposals, strong suggestion.

722110 望 wàng: at, call on, expect, full moon, gaze into the distance, hate, hope, look at, look forward, look into the distance, look over, look towards, prestige, reputation, resent, stare, to, towards, visit, wish.

722210 靖 jīng, jìng: appease, calm, make tranquil, pacify, peaceful, quiet, tranquil.

722300 湻 chuí, hún, zhuāng: merge, undifferentiated.

724500 辩 (辯) biàn, pián: adept at talk, argue, debate, discuss, dispute, distinguish, handle, manage.

nemonik-thinking.org

725020 解 jiě, jiè, xiè: acrobatic display on horseback, break up, comprehend, counteract, dissection, dissolve, divide, emancipate, explain, know, loosen, melt, open, relieve, remove, separate, solution, solve, split, transport under guard, understand, unfasten, untangle, untie.

725210 寡 guǎ: alone, bland, few, friendless, lack, widowed.

726101 毂 (轂) gū, gǔ: cart, hub of wheel, nave, wheel.

726101 锻 (鍛) duàn: discipline, forge metal, refine, temper - metal, toughen, work out, wrought.

726201 縠: Mentioned in some versions, but replaced with the simplified 222200 谷.

726310 辙 (轍) chè, zhé: remove, rhyme, rut, track, wagon ruts, way, wheel tracks, withdraw.

726310 辙迹 chèjì, zhéjì: rut, See 辙 track & 迹 footprint = trail, trail.

731110 请 (請) qīng, qíng, qǐng, qìng: ask, employ, engage, entertain, hire, invite, please, request, treat - to meal etc.

731210 猒 yā, yān, yàn: disgust.

nemonik-thinking.org

732020 堕 (墮) duò, huī: decay, degenerate, downhill, fall, fall into, sink.

732020 隋 suí: offal, residual meat.

732200 督 dū: army title, direct, oversee, supervise, supervise.

732210 精 jīng, jìng, qíng: bright, carefully, choice, demon, elite, energy, essence, excellent, extract, extremely fine, extremity, fine, highly perfected, mythical goblin spirit, perfect, physical and mental energy, precise, proficient - refined ability, quintessence, refined, selected rice, semen, sharp, skilled, smart, sperm, spirit, very, vitality.

732210 阗 (闐) tián: fill, fill the air with noise, fill up, full, grand, rumbling sound, terribly noisy.

734020 骋 (騁) chěng: gallop, give free rein, hasten, open up, run.

734300 憺 dàn: anxious, calm, composed, concerned, dread, fear, peace, peaceful, quiet, safely, self-possessed, shake, shock, stable, tranquil, worried.

734330 燬 huī: decay, destroy, overthrow, ruin.

741000 埴 tián, zhí: clay, clayey soil, clayey soil - unproductive, complete, fill - mould, fill a gap, fill in a form, mould, soil with large clay content.

741011 靓 (靚) jìng, liàng: attractive, beautiful - dress, dress, good-looking, handsome, make up - face, motionless, ornament, pretty, quiet.

742100 智 zhī, zhì: intelligence, knowledge, knowledgeable, known, wisdom, wit.

742100 智慧 zhìhuì: bright, clever, intelligent, knowledge, wisdom.

742100 智者 zhìzhě: clever and knowledgeable person, sage, wise man.

742110 弹 (彈) dàn, tán: accuse, ball, bomb, bullet, catapult, cross ball, elastic – material, flexible, flick, flip, fluff or tease cotton, impeach, lash out, leap, pellet, play - string instrument, pluck string, shell, shoot - catapult, shot, spring or leap, tease – wool.

742110 損: Mentioned in some versions, but replaced with the simplified 442110 损.

742200 僮 tóng, zhuàng: boy, boy servant, child, childish, degrading, houseboy, humble, ignorant, low, naïve, page - servant, servant-girl, slave girl, young.

742200 辟 (闢) bì, mǐ, pī, pì: avoid, break ground, develop, emperor, incisive, king, law, monarch, open up, open up land, penal law, penetrate, refute, repudiate, royal, rule, ward off, withdraw.

743110 跨 kù, kuā, kuǎ, kuà: adhere, bestride, carry, ride, span - bridge, step across, step astride, straddle, stride over, surpass.

744100 鲜 (鮮) xiān, xiǎn, xiàn: aquatic food, attractive, bright - colour, clear, delicacy, delicious, die - young, few, fresh, fresh - food, gaily-coloured, lack, little, live fish, rare, seldom, short of, special, tasty.

744400 鮮: Mentioned in some versions, but replaced with the simplified 744100 鲜.

751410 薄 báo, bó, bò, bù: approach, belittle, cold in manner, despise, frivolous, go near, indifferent, infertile, light, little, look down on, meagre, mean, peppermint, poor, slight, small, stingy, thin, ungenerous, unkind, weak.

752100 富 fù: abundant, ample, rich, wealthy.

752100 富贵 (富貴) fùguì: honour, influential, rich.

761200 福 fú, fù: assist, blessing, bow, complement, correspond, filled, fortune, full, good fortune, good

nemonik-thinking.org

luck, happiness, help, luck, match, prosperity, suit of clothes.

761210 槁 gǎo, kào: beat, dead, destroy, devastate, die, draft, dry, express regards, hit, manuscript, reward with food and drink, rotten - wood, rough copy, skinny, strike, thin, wither, withered, wreck.

762110 强 (強) jiàng, qiáng, qiǎng: barely, better, difficulty, dominate, energetic, firmly, force, grudgingly, make an effort, manage with effort, moral or intellectual strength, of high degree, physically strong, power, powerful, reluctantly, slightly more than, strive, strong, stubborn, unconvincing, unwillingly, unyielding, use force, vigorous, violent.

762110 强大 (強大) qiángdà: formidable, large, powerful, strong.

762110 强梁者 (強梁者) qiángliángzhě: brutal, bully, ruffian, strong violent person, surly, tyrannical, violent.

762110 强行 (強行) qiángxíng: break, force.

764101 憯 cǎn: already, crushing, disastrous, miserable, nevertheless, pitiful, sad, serious, sorrowful, wretched.

766400 耀 yào: brilliant, dazzle, glorious, glory, shine, show one's strength and power, sparkle.

767200 蹶 jué, juě, guì: fall down, kick as a horse, kick of horse, overthrown, stumble, trample, trip.

800000

823100 殖 shì, zhí: accumulate, breed, engage in trade, grow, increase, interest, multiply, prosper, putrefy, reproduce, reproduction, spawn.

824110 腹 fù: abdomen, belly, inside, stomach.

825400 澹 dàn: calm, placid, quiet, tranquil

833200 楗 jiǎn, jiàn: bar of door, bolt, bolt of lock, door, door lock, pile, post.

835100 镇 (鎮) zhèn: composed, cool, cool or chill - food or drinks, country town, garrison, guard, keep down, market place, post, press down, repress, small town, suppress, town.

841010 朝 cháo, zhāo, zhū: direct, dynasty, face, facing, government, imperial or royal court, make a pilgrimage, morning, palace, reign of a sovereign or emperor, towards.

841010 腊 (臘) là, xī: 12th moon of the lunar year - December, cured meat, dried meat, preserved meat, sacrifice, salted and dried, seventh day after birth, year-end sacrifice.

nemonik-thinking.org

843100 嗄 á, shà: exclamatory particle - ah - eh, hoarse voice, interjection expressing doubt or requiring answer, show realization, stress, what.

843200 積: Mentioned in some versions, but replaced with the simplified 333200 积.

843220 隨: Mentioned in some versions, but replaced with the simplified 633220 随.

844210 噭 jiào: allow, ask, beg, bid, boundary, call, cry, greet, hire, inspection tour, limitations, male-animal, name, obstacle, order, permit, shout.

846301 嘠 gā: creak, hoarse, screech.

852210 牖 yǒu: enlighten, lattice window, lead enlightenment, window.

860000 罪 zuì: blame, crime, evil, fault, guilt, hardship, sin, suffer, vice.

861000 置 zhì: buy, install, lay out, place, put, set aside, set up.

862000 辐 (輻) fú: radiate, spoke of a wheel.

864100 橐 tuó: air-blower, bag, bag opening at both ends, bird, click-clack sound, sack, sound of footsteps, tube for blowing fire, tube open at both ends.

864100 槖籥与 (槖籥與) tuóyuèyú, tuóyuèyǔ, tuóyuèyù: bagpipe.

875100 覆 fù: again, ambush, assault, capsize, check, cover, destroy, duplicate, go back, hatch, incubate, investigate, overflow, overturn, protect, reply, return, shelter, tip over.

875100 覆: Mentioned in some versions, but replaced with the simplified 523100 复.

875300 繟 chǎn: ease, frankly, generous, simple.

881010 鄙 bǐ: base, crude, despise, disdain, humble, look down upon, low, mean, rude, rustic, scorn.

883200 藏 cáng, zāng, zàng: accumulate, Buddhist or Taoist scripture, collect, conceal, depository, harbour, hide away, hoard, store, store up, storehouse.

884310 飄: Mentioned in some versions, but replaced with the simplified 653310 飘.

900000

914200 輿 (興) yú: area, carriage, cart, chariot, palanquin, popular, public, sedan chair, territory, world.

931201 慧 huì: bright, intelligent.

931211 龍: Mentioned in some versions, but replaced with the simplified 102101 龙.

nemonik-thinking.org

932020 静 (靜) jìng: admonish, calm, chaste, clean, facts, gentle, good, motionless, not moving, peaceful, pure, put in order, quiet, silent, sober, sort out, stabilize, still, tired, tranquil, unmoving, unstirred.

932100 肆 sì, tì: excess, four, four - banker's anti-fraud numeral, indulge, market, numeral four, particle meaning - now, shop, therefore, unbridled, unrestrained, wanton.

932220 靜: Mentioned in some versions, but replaced with the simplified 932020 静.

942100 瑕 xiá: blemish, defect, fault, flaw, flaw in a piece of jade, flaw in gem, shortcoming, slight blemish.

942100 瑕适 (瑕適) xiáshì: dot on jade, flaw, small blemish.

942111 醇 chún: alcohol, good wine, mellow wine, pure, rich, spirit, sterols, unmixed, wine with high alcohol content.

942111 醇醇 chúnchún: very pure.

943310 籌: Mentioned in some versions, but replaced with the simplified 603310 筹.

943311 羸 léi: emaciated, entangled, lean, skinny, thin, weak.

944101 觳: Mentioned in some versions, but replaced with the simplified 726101 縠.

945210 皦 jiǎo: bright - light, clear, distinct, pure, sparkling, white.

949600 纓: Mentioned in some versions, but replaced with the simplified 349300 缨.

951010 望 wàng: 15th day of month - lunar calendar, expect, gaze, hope, look.

952210 臂 bì, bei, bèi: arm, limb.

952300 璧 bì: jade annulus, round flat piece of jade with hole in centre used for ceremonial purposes.

953311 贏 (赢) yíng: beat, gain, profit, surplus, victory, win.

962300 譬 pì: example, for example, give an example, like, metaphor, simile.

963110 攫 jué: catch, grab, seize, snatch.

963110 攫鸟 juéniǎo: bird, bird of prey.

971010 彊 jiāng, jiàng, qiáng, qiǎng: compel, difficult, force, power, strong, strong power, stubborn, superior, uncompromising, wilful.

972000 霝 líng, lìng: drops of rain, fall in drops, medical herb, wither and fall.

972200 蹱 chòng, zhōng: act, bump, conduct, doddered, fall, jolt, move, stagger, toss.

974210 攘 níng, ráng, rǎng, ràng, xiǎng: arm, bare, bounce in, dispel, exclude, perturb, push up one's sleeves, reject or resist, remove, repel, roll up one's sleeve, seize, snatch, steal, surmount, take by force, throw into confusion.

974210 攘臂 rǎngbì: bare one's arms in agitation, push up one's sleeves and bare one's arms.

975330 鬻 jū, yù, zhōu, zhǔ, zhù: child, childish esp. in strained circumstances, nourish, sell, vending.

975330 鬻人 yùrén: sales people.

981200 器 qì: ability, article, bodily organ, capability, capacity, container, cup, device, implement, musical instrument, organ - body, receptacle, regard, talent, think highly of someone, tool, utensil, vessel, ware.

990000 圖: Mentioned in some versions, but replaced with the simplified 322300 图.

991000 儡 léi, lěi, kuǐ: decline, downfall, dummy, fail, frail, injure, over-worked, puppet, ruin, run-down, thin, tired, undermine, weak.

991000 儡儡 léiléi: very tired.

992100 躁 zào: agitated, excited, hot-tempered, impatient, irritable, rash, tense.

992200 趮 zào: cruel, easily provoked, fierce, hasty, impatient, impetuous, rash, restless.

993000 斲 zhuó: carve, carve wood, chop, cut, hack, polish.

993310 籥 yuè: flute, insert, instrument shaped like a flute, key, pipe, woodwind instrument.

996210 儽 léi, lěi: convict, dejected, detain, dispirited, fatigued, lazy, listless, overworked, prisoner, run-down, take into custody, tired, worn.

老子之

道德經

Lao Zi's

Dao De Jing

ENGLISH-CHINESE DICTIONARY

LAO ZI'S DAO DE JING

Legend

Line sequence: English meaning - *Digital Index for Pictographs (DIP)* – simplified pictograph (traditional pictograph) – Pinyin.

-A-

All-things: 201010 万物 (萬物) wànwù.

Ancients: 330000 古 gǔ.

-B-

Balance: 213110 均 jūn, yùn.

Benevolence: 211000 仁 rén.

-C-

Chi: See Qi.

Ci: See Qi.

Classic: 31860 經 jīng.

Compassion: 109501 慈 cí.

Competence: See Way of People.

Crowd: See Multitude.

-D-

Dao De Jing: 633300 道德經 (道德經) Dàodéjīng.

Dao: See Way of Nature.

DaoDeJing: See Dao De Jing.

Daodejing: See Dao De Jing.

De: See Way of People.

Desolate: 452100 萧 (蕭) xiāo.

Divide: See Name.

Downward: See Valley.

-E-

Earth: 122011 地 de, dì.

Efficiency: 201001 无为 (無為) wúwéi.

Effort: 630010 事 shì.

Emptiness: See Empty.

Empty: 331100 冲 (沖, 衝) chōng.

Energy of the universe: See Qi.

Equilibrium: See Balance.

Eternal Downward Force: 222200 谷神不死 gǔshēnbùsǐ.

Eternal: See Immortal.

Existence: 411010 有 yǒu, yòu.

-F-

Father: 002200 父 fǔ, fù.

Force of the universe: See Qi.

Force: See Spirit.

Four Greatnesses: 221001 四大 sìdà.

Frugality: 651100 啬 (嗇) sè.

Fu Yi (version of Dao De Jing): 541210 傅奕 Fu Yi.

-G-

Gravity: See Eternal Downward Force and Mysterious female.

Great Image: 101100 大象 dàxiàng.

Great Road: 101100 大道 dàdào.

Great: 101100 大 dà, dài, tài.

Greatnesses: See Great.

Guodian (version Dao De Jing): 533120 郭店 Guōdiàn.

-H-

Harmony: 332100 和 hé, hè, huó, huò & 531100 相 xiāng, xiàng.

Heaven: See Sky.

He-Shang Gong (version of Dao De Jing): 431210 河上公 Heshanggong.

Humbleness: See Not daring to act as the world's first.

Humility: See Not daring to act as the world's first.

-I-

Immortal Valley Spirit: See Eternal Downward Force.

Immortal: 111100 不死 bùsǐ.

Incompetence: 111100 不善 bùshàn.

Infiniteness: 410110 寻寻 xúnxún.

-J-

Justice: 001200 义 (義) yì.

-K-

King: 310000 王 wáng, wàng, yù.

Knowledge: 242200 贤 (賢) xián.

-L-

Lao Tse: See Lao Zi.

Lao Tsu: See Lao Zi.

Lao Tzu: See Lao Zi.

Lao Zi: 212001 老子 Lǎozi, Lǎozǐ.

Lao Zi's Dao De Jing: 212001 老子之道德經
    LǎozǐzhīDàodéjīng.

LaoTse: See Lao Zi.

Laotse: See Lao Zi.

LaoTsu: See Lao Zi.

Laotsu: See Lao Zi.

LaoTzu: See Lao Zi.

Laotzu: See Lao Zi.

LaoZi: See Lao Zi.

Laozi: See Lao Zi.

-M-

Master Carpenter: 101100 大匠 dàjiàng.

nemonik-thinking.org

Mawangdui (version of Dao De Jing): 302010 马王堆 (馬王堆) Mǎwángduī.

Moderation: 201001 无极 (無極) wújí.

Mother: 301210 母 mú, mǔ, wú, wǔ.

Multitude: 003300 众 (眾), 衆 zhòng.

Mysterious Female: 104200 玄牝 xuánpìn.

-N-

Name: 322100 名 míng.

Named: See Name.

Nameless: 201001 无名 (無名) wúmíng.

Naming: See Name.

Nature: See Sky.

Non-action: See Efficiency.

Non-existence: 201001 无 (無) mó, wú & 201001 无有 wúyòu.

Not daring to act as the world's first: 111100 不敢为天下先 bùgǎnwéitiānxiàxiān.

Nothingness: 201001 无物 (無物) wúwù.

-O-

One: 100000 一 yī.

Oneness: See One.

-P-

People: 001100 人 rén.

Physics: See Way of Nature.

Procrastination: 534202 稽 jī, qǐ.

Propriety: 111201 礼 (禮) lǐ.

Psychology: See Way of People.

-Q-

Qi: 311100 气 (氣) qì.

-R-

Restoration: 531100 相 xiāng, xiàng.

River sage: See He-Shang Gong.

River: 021000 川 chuān.

-S-

Sages: 311100 圣人 (聖人) shèngrén.

Simplicity: 121200 朴 (樸) piáo, pō, pò, pú, pǔ.

Singularity: See One.

Sky: 201100 天 tiān.

Spirit: 441200 神 shēn, shén.

Straw dogs: 41200 刍狗 chúgǒu.

Superior virtue: 21000 上德 shàngdé.

-T-

Tao Te Ching: See Dao De Jing.

nemonik-thinking.org

Tao—See Way of People.

TaoTeChing: See Dao De Jing.

Taoteching: See Dao De Jing.

Te: See De.

Three treasures: 300000 三宝 sānbǎo.

Tranquillity: 932020 静 (靜) jìng.

Two: 200000 二 èr.

-U-

Undivided: See One.

Universe: 530100 国 (國) guó.

-V-

Vacuum: See Empty and Nothingness.

Valley: 222200 谷 (穀) gòu, gǔ, hún, lù, nòu, yù.

Virtue: See Way of People.

Vital energy: See Qi.

Void: See Empty and Nothingness.

-W-

Wang Bi (version of Dao De Jing): 310000 王弼 Wángbì.

Water: 102110 水 shuǐ.

Way of Nature: 633300 道 dǎo, dào.

Way of People: 454201 德 dé.

Way: See Way of Nature.

nemonik-thinking.org

-X-

-Y-

Yang: 431010 阳 (陽) yáng.

Yin: 412020 阴 (陰) ān, yīn, yìn.

-Z-

Zero: See Empty and Nothingness.

nemonik-thinking.org

Yin-Yang

APPENDIX

nemonik-thinking.org

BIBLIOGRAPHY

A Comprehensive Chinese-English Dictionary. (2004). ISBN 7561124090: Dalian University of Technology Press.

A Dictionary of Chinese Proverbs etc. (1991). ISBN 7313008082/H31: Shanghai Jiao Tong University Press.

A Modern Chinese-English Dictionary. (2001). ISBN 9787560021881: Foreign Language Teaching and Research Press.

A New Century Classified Chinese-English Dictionary. (2003). ISBN 9787309034585: Fudan University Press.

A Reverse Chinese-English Dictionary. (1993). Beijing: The Commercial Press.

Chan Wing-Tsit. (1988). *The Way of Lao Tzu (Tao-te ching).* New York: Macmillan Publishing Company.

Cheng Gia-Fu and English, J. (1972). *Lao Tzu: Tao Te Ching.* New York: Vintage Books.

Chik Hon Man & Ng Lam Sim Yuk (ed.). (2001). *Chinese-English Dictionary.* Hong Kong: The Chinese University Press.

Collins. (2006). *Chinese Dictionary* (2 ed.). HarperCollins Publishers.

Collins. (2009). *Mandarin Chinese Dictionary* (1 ed.). HarperCollins Publishers.

nemonik-thinking.org

DeFrancis, John (ed.). (1996). *ABC Chinese-English Dictionary.* ISBN 9780824817442: University of Hawaii Press.

Fu Yi. (~200 BC). *See: Appendix / Chinese versions Dao De Jing / Fu Yi.*

Guodian. (~300 BC). *See: Appendix / Chinese versions Dao De Jing / Guodian.*

Henricks, R. G. (1993). *Lao-Tzu: Te-Tao Ching.* The modern library, New York.

He-Shang Gong. (179-157 BC). *See: Appendix / Chinese versions Dao De Jing / He-Shang Gong.*

Kleeman, J. (ed.). (2003). *Oxford Chinese Dictionary.* Oxford: Oxford University Press.

Land, P. (1990). *Lao Tsu: My Tao.* Puriri Press. Auckland, New Zealand.

Lao Zi. (~300 BC / sealed to 1993). *Guodian versions A, B, and C of Lao Zi's Dao De Jing.* Appendix / Chinese versions Dao De Jing / Guodian.

Lao Zi. (179-157 BC). *He-Shang Gong version of Lao Zi's Dao De Jing.* Appendix / Chinese versions Dao De Jing / He-Shang Gong.

Lao Zi. (206 BC / sealed 168 Bc to 1973). *Mawangdui version (A) of Lao Zi's Dao De Jing.* Appendix / Chinese versions Dao De Jing / Mawangdui (A).

nemonik-thinking.org

Lao Zi. (206 BC / sealed 168 Bc to 1973). *Mawangdui version (B) of Lao Zi's Dao De Jing.* Appendix / Chinese versions Dao De Jing / Mawangdui (B).

Lao Zi. (226-249 AD). *Wang Bi version of Lao Zi's Dao De Jing.* Appendix / Chinese versions Dao De Jing / Wang Bi.

Lao Zi. (555-639 AD / sealed ~200 BC). *Fu Yi version of Lao Zi's Dao De Jing.* Appendix / Chinese versions Dao De Jing / Fu Yi.

Lao Zi. (80 BC-10 AD). *Yan Sun version of Lao Zi's Dao De Jing.* http://www.reference.com/browse/Tao_Te_Ching.

Lau, D. C. (1985). *Lao Tzu: Tao Te Ching.* Penguin Books Ltd., London, England.

Liang Derun & Zheng Jiande. (1999). *Zhongda Chinese-English Dictionary.* Hong Kong: The Chinese University Press.

Lin Yutang. (1972). *Chinese-English Dictionary of Modern Usage.* Hong Kong: The Chinese University of Hong Kong.

Lin, J. P. (1977). *A Translation of Lao Tzu's Tao Te Ching and Wang Pi's commentary.* The University of Michigan.

Man-ho Kwok; Palmer, M.; & Ramsay, J. (1997). *Lao Tzu: The Tao Te Ching.* Element Books. Australia.

Manser, Martin H. (1999). *Concise English-Chinese & Chinese-English Dictionary.* Hong Kong: Oxford University Press.

Mawangdui (A). (~200 BC). *See: Appendix / Chinese versions Dao De Jing / Mawangdui-A.*

Mawangdui (B). (~200 BC). *See: Appendix / Chinese versions Dao De Jing / Mawangdui-B.*

Moss W. W. & Haitsma G. A. (2005). *New Age Chinese-English Dictionary.* ISBN 9787100043458: The Commercial Press.

New Chinese-English Lexicon. (1996). ISBN 201021141/Z47: Tianjin People's Publishing House.

Schade, A. (2016). *Dictionary Nemonik Thinking.* nemonik-thinking.org.

Schade, A. (2016). *Education Kills Humanity.* nemonik-thinking.org.

Schade, A. (2016). *Global Warming is the Solution.* nemonik-thinking.org.

Schade, A. (2016). *Glossary Nemonik Thinking.* nemonik-thinking.org.

Schade, A. (2016). *The Threat of Bilateral Climate Change.* nemonik-thinking.org.

Schade, A. (2016). *Think Smarter with Nemonik Thinking.* nemonik-thinking.org.

Schade, A. (2017). *Lao Tzu's Tao Te Ching* (2 ed.). nemonik-thinking.org.

Schade, A. (2017). *Lao Zi's Dao De Jing* (2 ed.). nemonik-thinking.org.

Schade, A. (2017). *Lao Zi's Dao De Jing Demystified* (2 ed., Vol. 4). nemonik-thinking.org.

Schade, A. (2017). *Lao Zi's Dao De Jing for Nemonik Thinkers* (2 ed.). nemonik-thinking.org.

Schade, A. (2017). *Stunning Revelations about Lao Zi's Dao De Jing* (2 ed., Vol. 5). nemonik-thinking.org.

Schade, A. (2018). *Dictionary Lao Zi's Dao De Jing* (1 ed., Vol. 1). nemonik-thinking.org.

Schade, A. (2018). *Meta-translation Lao Zi's Dao De Jing (1-37)* (2 ed., Vol. 2). nemonik-thinking.org.

Schade, A. (2018). *Meta-translation Lao Zi's Dao De Jing (38-81)* (2 ed., Vol. 3). nemonik-thinking.org.

Schade, A. (planned). *Sun Zi's The Art of War*. nemonik-thinking.org.

The New Chinese-English Dictionary. (2003). ISBN 9787313032522: Shanghai Jiao Tong University Press.

Times. (1999). *English-Chinese Dictionary*. Times Media Private Limited.

Waley, A. (1968). *Lao Tzu: The Way and its Power*. Mandala Books, London.

Wang Bi. (226-249 AD). *See: Appendix / Chinese versions Dao De Jing / Wang Bi.*

Wing, R. L. (1986). *Lao Tzu: The Tao of Power*. The Aquarian Press, London.

nemonik-thinking.org

Wu Guanghua. (2003). *A Comprehensive Chinese-English Dictionary*. Dalian University of Technology Press Pub.

nemonik-thinking.org

EXAMPLES DIP

一 丨 ／ ＼ 亅 乚

丶	000100 (any length)
丿	001000 (straight or curved)
儿	001001 (001000 straight or curved)
人	001100 (straight or curved)
灬	001300 (any length)
犭	002010 (000010 straight or curved)
从	002200 (straight or curved)
彡	003000 (straight or curved)
𠃌	005000 (any slope)
一	100000
乙	100001 (000001 straight or curved)
十	110000
阝	111010 (000010 straight or curved)
木	111100 (001100 straight or curved)
风	112200 (010100 two separate strokes)
二	200000
口	220000
四	221001
三	300000

nemonik-thinking.org

MY OTHER BOOKS

Dictionary Nemonik Thinking [1 of 3]

We need clear definitions to communicate. However, definitions associated with the mind and reality are inherently hypothetical, fuzzy, and intertwined. Therefore, the first part of this dictionary translates nemonik concepts into common keywords (e.g. *advance* into attack, bypass, etc.). In contrast, the second part translates common keywords into nemonik concepts (e.g. attack, bypass, etc. into *advance*). Nemonik thinking will improve your life. It accelerates your thinking; improves your memory; mobilizes your subconscious genius; strengthens your weaknesses; and reveals opportunities and threats. It helps you to pursue your goals in the right state of mind; at the right place, at the right time, with the right resources; and the right information. Nemonik thinking will assist you to think on your feet and become panic resistant during emergencies. Nemonik thinking is simple to learn, but it so sophisticated that it will make you a superior problem solver. Nemonik thinkers evaluate a checklist of seventeen nemoniks for each situation. Nemoniks are memorized keywords describing all aspects of your mind, reality, and their interaction (Schade, Think Smarter with Nemonik Thinking, 2016).

Free eBook @
nemonik-thinking.org

We need clear definitions to communicate. However, definitions associated with the mind and reality are inherently hypothetical, fuzzy, and intertwined. Therefore, this glossary attempts to provide definitions of the main concepts associated with nemonik thinking. Nemonik thinking will improve your life. It accelerates your thinking; improves your memory; mobilizes your subconscious genius; strengthens your weaknesses; and reveals opportunities and threats. It helps you to pursue your goals in the right state of mind; at the right place, at the right time, with the right resources; and the right information. Nemonik thinking will assist you to think on your feet and become panic resistant during emergencies. Nemonik thinking is simple to learn, but it so sophisticated that it will make you a superior problem solver. Nemonik thinkers evaluate a checklist of seventeen nemoniks for each situation. Nemoniks are memorized keywords describing all aspects of your mind, reality, and their interaction (Schade, Think Smarter with Nemonik Thinking, 2016).

Free eBook @
nemonik-thinking.org

Think Smarter with Nemonik Thinking [3 of 3]

Nemonik thinking will improve your life. It accelerates your thinking; improves your memory; mobilizes your subconscious genius; strengthens your weaknesses; and reveals opportunities and threats. It helps you to pursue your goals in the right state of mind; at the right place, at the right time, with the right resources; and the right information. Nemonik thinking will assist you to think on your feet and become panic resistant during emergencies. Nemonik thinking is simple to learn, but it so sophisticated that it will make you a superior problem solver. Nemonik thinkers evaluate a checklist of seventeen nemoniks for each situation. Nemoniks are memorized keywords describing all aspects of your mind, reality, and their interaction. Nemonik thinking is like playing a musical keyboard with seventeen keys producing an infinite repertoire of practical strategies. Nemonik thinking provides the strategic options for any possible situation, while Lao Zi's *Dao De Jing* provides the principle that identifies which of those options will fit the actual situation (Schade, Stunning Revelations about Lao Zi's Dao De Jing, 2017). The resulting strategies will maximize your success, which is to obtain what you seek and escape what you suffer. You might be the best thinker in the world, but only nemonik thinking could make you the smartest thinker you can be.

Free eBook @
nemonik-thinking.org

The Basics of Nemonik Mindpower

This is a crucial shortcut to a significant increase in your mindpower. You only have to memorize seventeen simple keywords called nemoniks that describe the mind, reality, and their interaction. Although simple, those nemoniks create a butterfly effect that will keep improving your mind forever. Without effort, they will accelerate your thinking, improve your memory, mobilize your hidden genius, turn your weaknesses into strengths, reveal opportunities and threats, and prepare you for emergencies. Pursue your goals in the right frame of mind. Nemonik thinking will make you the best thinker you can be.

Free eBook @
nemonik-thinking.org

nemonik-thinking.org

Dictionary Lao Zi's *Dao De Jing* [1 of 5].

This Chinese-English and English-Chinese dictionary is especially compiled for the translation of Lao Zi's ancient book *Dao De Jing* (Schade, Meta-translation Lao Zi's Dao De Jing (1-37), 2018) and (Schade, Meta-translation Lao Zi's Dao De Jing (38-81), 2018). *Dao De Jing* means literally—*A Classic about the Way of Nature and the Way of People*. It aims to maximize your success, which is to obtain what you seek and escape what you suffer. Success is maximized by aligning the *Way of People* with the *Way of Nature* (Schade, Stunning Revelations about Lao Zi's Dao De Jing, 2017). The Chinese versions used in this study include— (Wang Bi, 226-249 AD); (He-Shang Gong, 179-157 BC); (Fu Yi, ~200 BC); (Mawangdui (A), ~200 BC); (Mawangdui (B), ~200 BC); and (Guodian, ~300 BC). Together, those versions contain about 1,600 different pictographs. Every language changes over time and, therefore, some of Lao Zi's ancient pictographs are not used anymore, while the meaning of others has changed. In addition, most modern Chinese pictographs have several English meanings that foster ambiguity. Therefore, the exhaustive English meanings for each pictograph were extracted from reputable sources. Furthermore, a system of *Digital Index for Pictographs (DIP)* is introduced that simplifies the digital classification of Chinese pictographs.

Free eBook @
nemonik-thinking.org

The title of Lao Zi's ancient book *Dao De Jing* means literally—*A Classic about the Way of Nature and the Way of People*. *Dao De Jing* aims to maximize your success, which is to obtain what you seek and escape what you suffer. Success is maximized by aligning the *Way of People* with the *Way of Nature* (Schade, Stunning Revelations about Lao Zi's Dao De Jing, 2017). Despite the great efforts, previous translations of *Dao De Jing* do not present an adequate understanding of that mysterious manuscript. In order to take optimal advantage of the expertise accumulated in such earlier studies, this meta-translation is based on an English meta-analysis and a Chinese meta-analysis. The English meta-analysis is based on the following English translations— (Chan Wing-Tsit, 1988); (Cheng Gia-Fu and English, J, 1972); (Henricks, 1993); (Land, 1990); (Lau, 1985); (Lin, J. P., 1977); (Man-ho Kwok; Palmer, M.; & Ramsay, J., 1997); (Waley, 1968); and (Wing, 1986). The Chinese meta-analysis is based on the following Chinese versions of *Dao De Jing*— (Wang Bi, 226-249 AD); (He-Shang Gong, 179-157 BC); (Fu Yi, ~200 BC); (Mawangdui (A), ~200 BC); (Mawangdui (B), ~200 BC); and (Guodian, ~300 BC). This meta-translation of Dao (Chapters 1-37) is based on a special dictionary (Schade, Dictionary Lao Zi's Dao De Jing, 2018), while it is the foundation for (Schade, Lao Zi's Dao De Jing Demystified, 2017).

Free eBook @
nemonik-thinking.org

The title of Lao Zi's ancient book *Dao De Jing* means literally—*A Classic about the Way of Nature and the Way of People.* *Dao De Jing* aims to maximize your success, which is to obtain what you seek and escape what you suffer. Success is maximized by aligning the *Way of People* with the *Way of Nature* (Schade, Stunning Revelations about Lao Zi's Dao De Jing, 2017). Despite the great efforts, previous translations of *Dao De Jing* do not present an adequate understanding of that mysterious manuscript. In order to take optimal advantage of the expertise accumulated in such earlier studies, this meta-translation is based on an English meta-analysis and a Chinese meta-analysis. The English meta-analysis is based on the following English translations— (Chan Wing-Tsit, 1988); (Cheng Gia-Fu and English, J, 1972); (Henricks, 1993); (Land, 1990); (Lau, 1985); (Lin, J. P., 1977); (Man-ho Kwok; Palmer, M.; & Ramsay, J., 1997); (Waley, 1968); and (Wing, 1986). The Chinese meta-analysis is based on the following Chinese versions of *Dao De Jing*— (Wang Bi, 226-249 AD); (He-Shang Gong, 179-157 BC); (Fu Yi, ~200 BC); (Mawangdui (A), ~200 BC); (Mawangdui (B), ~200 BC); and (Guodian, ~300 BC). This meta-translation of De (Chapters 38-81) is based on a special dictionary (Schade, Dictionary Lao Zi's Dao De Jing, 2018), while it is the foundation for (Schade, Lao Zi's Dao De Jing Demystified, 2017).

Free eBook @
nemonik-thinking.org

Lao Zi's *Dao De Jing* Demystified [4 of 5]

The title of Lao Zi's ancient book *Dao De Jing* means literally—*A Classic about the Way of Nature and the Way of People*. It aims to maximize your success, which is to obtain what you seek and escape what you suffer. Success is maximized by aligning the *Way of People* with the *Way of Nature*. The current study presents four English versions of increasing demystification. The first one is the *Meta-translation* version as developed in (Schade, Meta-translation Lao Zi's Dao De Jing (1-37), 2018) and (Schade, Meta-translation Lao Zi's Dao De Jing (38-81), 2018). However, Lao Zi's poetic style, mysticism, metaphors, and synonyms are still inhibiting a clear understanding. The second one is the *Clarification* version, which is presented in parallel with the *Meta-translation*. That clarification increased the consistency of Lao Zi's terminology, but significant chapters about *Dao* are still located in the *De* section and vice versa. Therefore, the third one is the *Chapters Reorganized* version in which the chapters are relocated to the *Dao* and *De* sections. Nevertheless, the text remains fuzzy, because several chapters relate to both sections. Therefore, the fourth one is the *Sentences Reorganized* version in which the sentences are sorted by topic. That version is the foundation for (Schade, Stunning Revelations about Lao Zi's Dao De Jing, 2017).

Free eBook @
nemonik-thinking.org

nemonik-thinking.org

The title of Lao Zi's ancient book *Dao De Jing* means in modern terminology—*A Classic about the Physics of Psychology.* *Dao De Jing* is a significant contribution of the Chinese literature to the contemporary sciences of physics and psychology. Lao Zi presents a sophisticated theory concerning the origin, formation, and working of the universe. Although that theory is at the cutting edge of modern physics, it provides a simple and practical principle. That principle holds that the unstoppable force *Qi* will always maintain the multitude of *Yin-Yang* balances comprising our universe. Therefore, Lao Zi's theory of psychology predicts that people can only maximize their success by aligning with *Qi.* Success is to obtain what you seek and escape what you suffer. Unfortunately, humanity has ignored Lao Zi's principles for two-and-halve thousand years. As a result, we are now facing manmade problems such as climate change, continuous warfare, dwindling resources, environmental pollution, and overpopulation. Those problems threaten your personal success and they cannot be solved with the same way of thinking that has created them. Therefore, Lao Zi's *Dao De Jing* is more relevant than ever. His way of dynamic thinking fosters solutions that reach peacefully across the fault-lines created by race, religion, and ideology. This book is based on (Schade, Lao Zi's Dao De Jing Demystified, 2017).

Free eBook @
nemonik-thinking.org

Lao Zi's *Dao De Jing* (Chinese-English)

Lao Zi's *Dao De Jing* or Lao Tzu's *Tao Te Ching* is a beautiful example of ancient Chinese literature. *Dao De Jing* means literally—*A Classic about the Way of Nature and the Way of People.* It aims to maximize your success, which is to obtain what you seek and escape what you suffer. Success is maximized by aligning the *Way of People* with the *Way of Nature.* After two-and-halve thousand years, Lao Zi's wisdom is still ahead of time and outshines intellectual giants such as Confucius, Sun Zi, Socrates, Plato, and Aristotle. Lao Zi's deep understanding of nature and people is your guiding light to a better future, because his way of dynamic thinking reaches peacefully across the fault-lines created by race, religion, and ideology. Therefore, *Dao De Jing* is more relevant than ever. This book comprises Chinese and English versions of *Dao De Jing*, which are extracted from (Schade, Lao Zi's Dao De Jing Demystified, 2017). Furthermore, Lao Zi's amazing secrets are revealed in (Schade, Stunning Revelations about Lao Zi's Dao De Jing, 2017).

Free eBook @
nemonik-thinking.org

Lao Tzu's *Tao Te Ching* (English)

Lao Tzu's *Tao Te Ching* or Lao Zi's *Dao De Jing* is a beautiful example of ancient Chinese literature. *Tao Te Ching* means literally—*A Classic about the Way of Nature and the Way of People.* It aims to maximize your success, which is to obtain what you seek and escape what you suffer. Success is maximized by aligning the *Way of People* with the *Way of Nature.* After two-and-halve thousand years, Lao Tzu's wisdom is still ahead of time and outshines intellectual giants such as Confucius, Sun Zi, Socrates, Plato, and Aristotle. Lao Tzu's deep understanding of nature and people is your guiding light to a better future, because his way of dynamic thinking reaches peacefully across the fault-lines created by race, religion, and ideology. Therefore, *Tao Te Ching* is more relevant than ever. This book comprises an English version of *Tao Te Ching*, which is extracted from (Schade, Lao Zi's Dao De Jing Demystified, 2017). Furthermore, Lao Tzu's amazing secrets are revealed in (Schade, Stunning Revelations about Lao Zi's Dao De Jing, 2017).

Free eBook @
nemonik-thinking.org

Lao Zi for Nemonik Thinkers

Lao Zi's *Dao De Jing* is the most significant contribution from ancient China to contemporary psychology. *Dao De Jing* means in modern terminology—*A Classic about the Physics of Psychology*. It aims to maximize your success, which is to obtain what you seek and escape what you suffer. Success is maximized by aligning psychology with the laws of physics. In accord, nemonik thinking aims to maximize your success by evaluating a checklist of seventeen nemoniks for each situation. Nemoniks are memorized keywords describing all aspects of your mind, reality, and their interaction (Schade, Think Smarter with Nemonik Thinking, 2016). Nemonik thinking provides the exhaustive strategic options for any possible situation, while *Dao De Jing* provides the principle that identifies which of those options will fit the actual situation. Although Lao Zi's holistic format enhances the mystery and poetic beauty of his amazing manuscript, it also reduces the effectiveness of *Dao De Jing* as a rational teaching tool. Therefore, I have used the nemonik template to restructure *Dao De Jing* for nemonik thinkers. Furthermore, Lao Zi's amazing secrets are revealed in (Schade, Stunning Revelations about Lao Zi's Dao De Jing, 2017).

Free eBook @
nemonik-thinking.org

nemonik-thinking.org

Education Kills Humanity

The aim of this study is to evaluate the educational system with nemonik thinking (Schade, Think Smarter with Nemonik Thinking, 2016). The system conditions students with certificates to maximize their probability of winning the educational competition. The winners are rewarded with advantageous positions in society, while the losers are doomed to serve the winners. Therefore, conventional thinking is conflict oriented, which fosters aggression, control, effort, and force. The conditioned compulsion to win arguments inhibits also the truth and, therefore, it corrupts conventional thinking. As a result, the educational system produces incompetent leaders and rebellious followers. That counterproductive combination fosters manmade problems such as climate change, continuous warfare, dwindling resources, environmental pollution, and overpopulation. Those problems cannot be solved with the same way of conventional thinking that has created them. In contrast, nemonik thinking aims for success, rather than winning. Success is to obtain what you seek and to escape what you suffer. Therefore, nemonik thinking is goal oriented, which fosters freedom, alignment, compassion, allies, and win-win strategies. You might be the best thinker in the world, but only nemonik thinking could make you the smartest thinker you can be. This book contains extracts from (Schade, Think Smarter with Nemonik Thinking, 2016).

Free eBook @
nemonik-thinking.org

Global Warming is the Solution

The aim of this study is to accelerate the development of climatology with nemonik thinking (Schade, Think Smarter with Nemonik Thinking, 2016). About 400,000 years of data, extracted from the Antarctic Vostok ice-core, were subjected to statistical analyses. The results suggest that the duration and thermal stability of the current interglacial are significantly larger than those of the four previous ones are. Hence, the results could not be contributed to natural variables. This supports the hypothesis that the current interglacial period changed some time ago into a glacial period, while artificial global warming has compensated for that natural global cooling. During a glacial period, the average global atmospheric temperature could decrease with about 10.0 °C. This would reduce the global food supply; threaten the global infrastructure; and force billions of people to migrate back towards the equator. Therefore, artificial global warming could be the solution for natural glacial cooling. Further research of this topic is crucial.

Free eBook @
nemonik-thinking.org

The Threat of Bilateral Climate Change

The aim of this study is to accelerate the development of climatology with nemonik thinking (Schade, Think Smarter with Nemonik Thinking, 2016). During the industrial period, the atmospheric CO_2 concentration has increased about 120 ppm, while the average global atmospheric temperature increased about 1.4 °C. However, the Vostok thermal function of CO_2 during the last 400,000 years predicts that the increase of 120 ppm of CO_2 would increase the temperature with 11.6 °C. Hence, there is a thermal gap of 10.2 °C between the observed and predicted temperature. This gap could be explained by the proposed bilateral hypothesis of climate change. This hypothesis holds that the observed increase in average global atmospheric temperature of 1.4 °C is the balance of an artificial global warming of 11.6 °C and a natural global cooling of 10.2 °C. Those large opposing thermal phenomena could explain the recent climatological instability. Furthermore, the bilateral hypothesis predicts that an uncontrolled decrease of atmospheric CO_2 could trigger glacial conditions threatening humanity. Therefore, further research of this topic is crucial. This book contains extracts of (Schade, Global Warming is the Solution, 2016).

Free eBook @
nemonik-thinking.org

Sun Zi's The Art of War (planned)

Sun Zi (554-496 BC) was a Chinese warrior-philosopher who wrote the military classic *Bing Fa* or *The Art of War*. Sun Zi applied Lao Zi's philosophy to the art of warfare (Schade, Stunning Revelations about Lao Zi's Dao De Jing, 2017). Similar to Lao Zi, the aim of Sun Zi is to maximize your success by constant positioning. Incompetent warriors will be forced to fight, because they fail to position themselves adequately. As a result, they will destroy their own resources and their potential spoils of war. Hence, a third party might take advantage of their weaknesses and defeat both opponents. Therefore, Sun Zi concludes that superior warriors do not fight. They will pursue the right goals, and are in the right place, at the right time, with the right resources and information, and in the right state of mind. Although Sun Zi's book is about war, his strategies apply to every facet of daily life. He addresses the questions raised by nemonik thinking of where, what, and when to advance, stay, retreat, accumulate, preserve, dispose, act, wait, prepare, accept, reject, reveal, and conceal (Schade, Think Smarter with Nemonik Thinking, 2016). Therefore, maximize your success by incorporating Sun Zi's strategies in your daily thinking.

Free eBook @
nemonik-thinking.org

WEBSITE

It is the aim of my website to provide interactive on-line information about nemonik thinking. This includes discussions, books, blog, videos, exercises, updates, activities, web links, and tests. Join the nemonik thinkers and receive the latest updates. It is a work in progress. Check it out and have your say. I look forward to your feedback at:

nemonik-thinking.org

www.ingramcontent.com/pod-product-compliance
Lightning Source LLC
Chambersburg PA
CBHW051043050726
47592CB00002B/367